"Professor Sandeep Goel, through his Forensic Accounting novella, provides an exciting and captivating introduction to the world of financial investigation and fraud detection. It is ideal for anyone who wants to gain extensive knowledge and professional skills in the related subject. A quality read for in-depth navigation to this fascinating field!"

—**Dr. James A. Gabriele,** *Professor of Accounting, Department of Accounting & Finance, Feliciano School of Business, Montclair State University, US*

"This engaging and supremely practical book is a must-read for anyone looking to understand the intricate world of financial frauds and forensic accounting, including analytics. With clear explanations, real-world examples, and insightful analysis, the book demystifies complex concepts and showcases how they can be applied in real-life scenarios."

—**Dr. Raman Garg**, *Indian Revenue Service (IRS), Commissioner of Income Tax, Ministry of Finance, GoI, New Delhi*

FORENSIC ACCOUNTING AND FINANCIAL SHENANIGANS DETECTION

This volume demystifies the mechanics of financial shenanigans or earnings management (EM) in the interests of investors and other stakeholders who are affected by corporate fiascos. It brings extensive real-world experience of forensic accounting and analytics capabilities to examine "financial hazards," how they inevitably result in financial and corporate blowups, and what lessons we can draw from them, such as those of Enron, WorldCom, Satyam Computers, Kingfisher Airlines, Lehman Brothers, and of late IL&FS, Silicon Valley Bank (SVB), and many more.

The book decodes:

- The nuances and intricacies of forensic accounting;
- Revenue, expense, and assets manipulation;
- Identification of "red flags" and quantitative analysis;
- Fraud prevention mechanics.

Richly illustrated with tables, figures, and learning tools, this volume will be indispensable for individuals, business managers, and management students pursuing courses related to forensic accounting, financial shenanigans, and financial ethics. It will also be an important resource for executive and management development programmes (EDPs & MDPs), as well as professionals, corporates, entrepreneurs, government officials, academicians, and researchers looking for a quick refresher on financial manipulations.

Sandeep Goel is Senior Professor of Accounting and Finance, and Corporate Governance at Management Development Institute (MDI), Gurgaon, India. He holds two doctorates, one in Finance; and another in Accounting from the Faculty of Management Studies, University of Delhi. He completed his bachelor's with Hons. and master's degrees in Commerce with specialisation in Finance from Shri Ram College of Commerce, and the Department of Commerce, Delhi School of Economics, University of Delhi, respectively. He has three decades of industry and academic experience across various organisations and institutions of repute, including the Shri Ram Group, the University of Delhi, and MDI Gurgaon. He sits as Independent Director on the Board of Machino Plastics Ltd., Gurugram, a Suzuki JV. He is Visiting Professor to the Faculty of Management, University of Lodz, Poland, and Aix-Marseille Graduate School of Management – IAE AIX – Marseille University, France. He is Management Trainer and Consultant to organisations like Maruti Suzuki, Canara Bank, JK Tyre, PFRDA, NPCI, IRS, ITS, FIA Business School (Brazil), Bata, Encore, Federal-Mogul Goetze (India) Ltd., SOS Village International, Cairns India, National Banking Institute (Nepal), Druk Holdings (Bhutan), UltraTech Cements, ONGC, and many more. He is a prolific writer and has authored more than 15 books and published over 100 research articles and cases in national and international journals of repute. He has been conferred with the Award for Excellence in Teaching, 2023-24, 2015–16, and Award for Excellence in Research, 2015–16 at MDI.

Foundations of Finance

Series author: **Sandeep Goel** is a Senior Professor of Accounting and Finance, and Corporate Governance, Management Development Institute (MDI) Gurgaon, India.

This series presents the foundations of financial knowledge in a lucid and accessible format. The books in the series deal with critical themes in financial literacy and proficiency today, such as financial accounting, cost accounting, corporate finance, contemporary finance, forensic accounting, fraud analytics, and fraud risk management. Each volume in the series deals with updated expert insights, current global trends, and real-world cases in finance and is richly illustrated with tables, figures, and learning tools. The individual books in the series will be indispensable for individuals, business managers, and management students pursuing undergraduate and postgraduate courses in finance. They will also be important resources for executive and management development programmes (EDPs & MDPs) as well as beginners and professionals interested in a short refresher course on finance and financial management.

Forensic Accounting and Financial Shenanigans Detection
Sandeep Goel

FORENSIC ACCOUNTING AND FINANCIAL SHENANIGANS DETECTION

Sandeep Goel

Routledge
Taylor & Francis Group
LONDON AND NEW YORK

Designed cover image: Getty Images

First published 2026
by Routledge
4 Park Square, Milton Park, Abingdon, Oxon OX14 4RN

and by Routledge
605 Third Avenue, New York, NY 10158

Routledge is an imprint of the Taylor & Francis Group, an informa business

British Library Cataloguing-in-Publication Data
A catalogue record for this book is available from the British Library

ISBN: 978-1-041-21227-0 (hbk)
ISBN: 978-1-041-22012-1 (pbk)
ISBN: 978-1-003-73018-7 (ebk)

DOI: 10.4324/9781003730187

Typeset in Sabon
by Deanta Global Publishing Services, Chennai, India

CONTENTS

FIGURES

TABLES

PREFACE

Over the years, the world has witnessed numerous cases of earnings manipulation, leading to corporate scandals and white-collar crime by people at the top. This has been a collaborative activity, rather than an individual effort, and is a serious, costly, and growing epidemic for business and government, and in particular for shareholders, and therefore calls for serious financial diligence – disrupting the silos of misconduct to foster real-world change for stakeholders' interests at large. This book intends to expose you to the world of forensic accounting and sails you through the world of financial manipulations, their early detection and prevention for the benefits of all.

It will help to develop not only an understanding of the foundation of accounting and financial shenanigans but, most importantly, to enable investors and common people to use it as an effective tool for financial investment, monitoring, analysis, and resource allocation. It is expected to be a useful resource for executive and management development programmes (EDPs & MDPs) oriented towards business executives, corporate managers, and management students, including MBA & allied programmes.

Organisation of the book

The book has been divided into six parts. It has been logically sequenced to facilitate better connectivity and learning among the readers. Most chapters are self-contained and can be read independently of the others.

Chapter 1, "Forensic accounting: Introduction," provides an introductory overview of forensic accounting.

Chapter 2, "Financial shenanigans/Earnings management (EM)," demystifies different forms of earnings manipulation conducted by business organisations in the world, including India.

Chapter 3, "Forensic analytics," exposes the accounting methods, tools, and techniques to detect these EM practices.

Chapter 4, "Financial shenanigans analyses and discussion," undertakes and recognises the real-world companies and examines the quality of their financial manipulation using given models.

Chapter 5, "Detection and prevention of financial frauds," approaches corporate financial statements' readability from a comprehensive perspective and deliberates financial challenges in detail.

Chapter 6, "Corporate fiascos," discusses prominent accounting frauds that occurred over the years, nationally and internationally.

Chapter 7, "Caselets," presents different caselets/examples on financial shenanigans and gimmicks.

This book will build up your forensic skills, which are essential not only for your rational investment(s) but also for your professional growth and success. I am confident that the readers will find this book truly valuable in terms of its quality and presentation. Any constructive comments and suggestions for future improvement of the book are highly appreciated and welcome at *sandeepgoel1810@gmail.com.*

Happy learning!

ACKNOWLEDGEMENTS

This book is the outcome of decades of rich experience in imparting forensic knowledge and skills to thousands of students and participants across different levels in corporates and organisations. At this moment, I take the opportunity to express my gratitude to all those whose inspiring queries and questions have motivated me to pen this single-window volume on "forensic accounting."

I wish to thank God Almighty for everything in life! The work would be incomplete if I do not acknowledge my parents' contribution. They have been a constant source of inspiration for me and have always stood by me through thick and thin. My wife provided her unstinting support and encouragement in completing the book. My daughter Maanya is my soul, whose smile always keeps me going in life.

I am also thankful to the entire team of Routledge, New Delhi, including Dr. Shashank Sinha, Mr. Yogesh Srivastava, and Ms. Anvitaa Bajaj, for their tremendous support and wholehearted cooperation at all stages of publication of this book.

My sincere thanks are also due to Professor James A. Gabriele and Dr. Raman Garg for their valuable support and endorsements of the book.

Last but not the least, I gratefully express my gratitude to the following fellow academic colleagues and professional associates for providing their invaluable advice and inputs for the enrichment of the book.

- **Dr Brian P. Miller**, *Professor of Accounting, Warrington College of Business, University of Florida, US*
- **Dr Robert C. Rickards**, *Professor of Accounting, German Police University, Münster, Germany*
- **Dr Maciej Turała**, *Vice Dean for International Relations, University of Lodz, Poland*
- **Mr S. S. Sharma**, *IAS Retd, Former Secretary, Government of India, Gurugram*
- **Dr J. P. Singh**, *Former Professor of Finance, Department of Management Studies, Indian Institute of Technology, Roorkee*
- **Mr Aditya Jindal**, *Chairman cum Managing Director, Machino Plastics Ltd., Gurugram*
- **Dr Niti Nandini Chatnani**, *Professor of Finance, Indian Institute of Foreign Trade, New Delhi*
- **Dr Sonam Chawla**, *Associate Professor of Organizational Behaviour, O.P. Jindal Global University, Sonipat*
- **Dr Vishakha Bansal**, *Assistant Professor of Finance & Control, Indian Institute of Management, Shillong*
- **Dr Ajay Kumar**, *Assistant Professor, Bharati Vidyapeeth Institute of Management & Research, New Delhi*

ABBREVIATIONS

AICPA	American Institute of Certified Public Accountants
AIG	American Insurance Group
AQI	Asset quality index
DACC	Discretionary accruals
DSRI	Day's sales in receivables index
EBIT	Earnings before interest and tax
EM	Earnings management
GAAP	Generally accepted accounting principles
GMI	Gross margin index
IL&FS	Infrastructure Leasing & Finance Services Limited
PAT	Profit after tax
PPE	Property plant and equipment
SEC	Securities and Exchange Commission
SGI	Sales growth index
SVB	Silicon Valley Bank
TACC	Total accruals
TATA	Total accruals to total assets

1

FORENSIC ACCOUNTING

The introduction

Detecting and preventing fraud was identified as a component of the accounting function by the internal and/or external auditors. However, it was later discovered that auditors only verify that a business entity's financial reporting is in compliance and are not tasked with looking into fraud. As a result, "forensic accounting," a new branch of accounting, was created to identify fraudulent activity occurring in corporate settings. Forensic accounting became necessary as corporate scandals became more frequent globally. The fall of Enron, WorldCom, and Parmalat brought about a global crisis that made it necessary to implement procedures and controls that were created by forensic accountants and auditors to identify, stop, and respond to frauds.[1] India is no exception with its own set of fiascos of Satyam, Kingfisher, and IL&FS, and many more. With a new kind of fraud being discovered every day, regardless of the regulatory measures, this has necessitated the development of forensic accounting expertise worldwide.

1.1 What is forensic accounting?

Forensic accounting involves the process of understanding, identifying, detecting, and communicating fraud patterns and schemes to stakeholders as a part of the investigation process. Accounting standards allow managers to exercise discretion in financial reporting. However, managerial discretion can be misused and used to commit and cover up fraud.

DOI: 10.4324/9781003730187-1

According to the American Institute of Certified Public Accountants (AICPA, 1993), "Forensic accounting is the application of accounting principles, theories, and discipline to facts or hypotheses at issues in a legal dispute and encompasses every branch of accounting knowledge."

Primarily, it involves the following three steps:

(a) how perpetrators engage in fraud
(b) how it manifests and is disguised
(c) how to detect fraud

In today's business environment, forensic accounting, as a specialised field of investigation into fraud or financial manipulation, becomes extremely valuable because it deals with a variety of financial issues and conflicts. It is a vital asset for organisations worldwide because of its importance in fraud detection, prevention, and business due diligence on a variety of financial matters for both individuals and businesses.

1.2 Role of forensic accounting

In the modern business world, forensic accountants or analysts are crucial because they apply their unique knowledge and skills to a range of financial investigations. In cases of financial misconduct, forensic accountants can help individuals and businesses protect their financial interests and pursue justice. The following responsibilities are a part of the job description for forensic accountants and investigators:

1.2.1 Fraud detection and prevention

Forensic accountants are experts in detecting and stopping fraudulent activity in companies. They use their accounting and auditing expertise in addition to their analytical skills to spot financial irregularities like embezzlement, financial statement fraud, and tax evasion. Furthermore, they help companies implement internal controls and processes that can help stop fraud before it begins.

1.2.2 Litigation support

Forensic accountants often offer litigation support in cases involving financial disputes. They provide expert witness testimony in court, review financial documents, and assist attorneys in understanding complex financial issues. Among other things, their opinions can be very useful in resolving disputes involving contracts, shareholder conflicts, and intellectual property.

1.2.3 Business valuation

The valuation of companies and assets is another area in which forensic accountants are highly skilled. They assess a company's or its assets' worth using their financial knowledge, which can be significant in situations involving estate planning, mergers and acquisitions, and many other things. Their extensive understanding of accounting principles and valuation techniques enables them to produce reliable and accurate valuations.

1.2.4 Bankruptcy and insolvency analysis

Businesses that are having financial difficulties can get in touch with forensic accountants to evaluate the situation and provide advice on bankruptcy and insolvency procedures. They examine the company's prior financial transactions, evaluate the feasibility of the business plan, and assess its ability to repay debt. Their findings can help interested parties make well-informed decisions about the company's future and create plans to address its financial issues.

1.2.5 Insurance claims

In the insurance business, forensic accountants assist in resolving claims involving monetary losses. Financial records are examined, the extent of damages is evaluated, and the right amount of compensation for policyholders is decided. They work together with investigators to protect insurance companies' interests and uncover suspected insurance fraud.

1.3 Skills and qualifications for forensic accountants

Forensic accountants act as a catalyst in detecting, investigating, and preventing fraud in businesses. To excel in this field, they must possess a unique set of skills and qualifications. The following section discusses five key areas that are essential for success in forensic accounting.

1.3.1 Accounting and auditing know-how

The core of forensic accounting is a strong foundation in accounting and auditing principles. Besides professional qualifications in accounting, forensic accountants must have a deep understanding of financial statements, generally accepted accounting principles (GAAP), and internal controls. This enables them to spot anomalies, evaluate dangers, and find possible fraud schemes.

1.3.2 Analytical ability

Forensic accountants need to be highly analytical and possess strong critical thinking skills. To uncover hidden patterns that result in fraud, they must be able to review financial records, spot irregularities, and evaluate complicated data. These professionals need to be able to identify financial crimes, investigate them, and determine the best course of action.

1.3.3 Detailed insight

A keen eye for detail is vital for forensic accountants, as even the smallest errors or inconsistencies can be critical in detecting fraud. They must properly review the financial records, ensuring that all transactions are properly documented and accounted for, and should prepare all reports and presentations.

1.3.4 Communication skills

Forensic accountants must be effective communicators, capable of presenting complex financial information in a clear and concise manner. They must be able to communicate their findings and conclusions in a way that non-accounting professionals can understand because they frequently interact with clients, lawyers, and law enforcement.

1.3.5 Legal expertise

Forensic accountants must possess a thorough understanding of the legal and regulatory framework surrounding financial crime and fraud. This implies being well acquainted with relevant laws, regulations, and industry standards in addition to staying up to date on the latest developments in white-collar crime. This information is necessary to comply with all applicable laws and regulations.

1.4 The forensic accounting process

The forensic accounting process is a systematic approach to uncovering financial fraud and providing litigation support. This process involves five key steps, each of which plays a crucial role in ensuring that the investigation is thorough and accurate.

1.4.1 Planning

During the planning phase, forensic accountants work closely with their clients to establish the scope of the investigation. This includes identifying the specific financial issues to be addressed, setting objectives for the investigation, and developing a comprehensive plan of action. This stage is critical, as it lays the foundation for the entire investigation and ensures that all parties involved are on common terms.

1.4.2 Data collection and analysis

Next, the forensic accountant collects and analyses financial data relevant to the case. This may involve examining financial statements, bank records, invoices, and other documentation to identify any discrepancies or signs of fraud. The accountant will use various techniques and tools, such as ratio analysis and data mining, to scrutinise the data and uncover any irregularities. This stage forms the basis of the accountant's findings and recommendations.

1.4.3 Reporting

Once the data has been collected and analysed, the forensic accountant prepares a detailed report outlining their findings. This report will include a summary of the investigation, the methodologies used, and the conclusions reached.

1.4.4 Presentation

The accountant might have to present their findings to their client, legal counsel, or other case stakeholders after completing the written report. This stage is essential since it entails providing the relevant stakeholders with an accurate and well-documented synopsis of the investigation's conclusions.

1.4.5 Litigation support and testimony

In certain situations, the forensic accountant's duties might go beyond the actual investigation and into the courtroom. When asked to testify as expert witnesses, forensic accountants may be required to offer the necessary litigation support and bolster a case for their clients. This contributes to establishing the case's legitimacy.

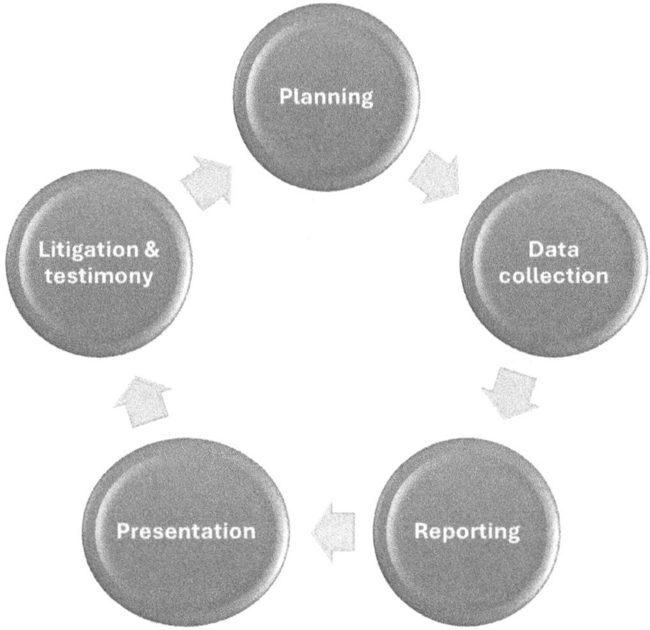

FIGURE 1.1 Forensic accounting process

Thus, the forensic accounting procedure is a methodical and exacting way to find financial fraud and support legal proceedings, as presented in Figure 1.1.

1.5 Grey zones in forensic accounting

*1.5.1 The signalling of discretionary accruals**

There is enough data to demonstrate that investors attempt to predict future earnings performance using the information at their disposal. Instead of earnings' capacity to condense

* Refer to Chapter 3 for the concept of discretionary accruals.

information that is relevant to value, it reflects investors' naive obsession with reported earnings.

The majority of analysts contend that since investors frequently "fixate" on reported earnings, mispriced securities can be identified by looking at the accrual and cash-flow components of current earnings. The rationale is that the evaluation of future earnings is affected differently by the accrual and cash-flow components of earnings. Discretionary choices in financial reporting that can ultimately lead to, or create, future earnings that drive stock prices must be identified and adjusted for. As a result, financial statement users must develop a keen understanding of the fundamentals and choices underlying each firm's business operations.

1.5.2 Corporate attitude

One or more of the following three methods used by corporations to manage earnings are: (i) selecting from the flexible options offered by GAAP, (ii) the application of choices and subjective estimates offered by the options, and (iii) using asset acquisitions and dispositions and the timing of their reporting.

It should be noted that decisions made outside of GAAP amount to fraud, whereas decisions made within GAAP amount to earnings management (EM) or financial shenanigans (manipulations). This is a concern. In certain situations, it becomes difficult to determine whether certain management reporting practices that deviate from GAAP constitute fraud or earnings management.

1.5.3 Behavioural bias

CEOs and other top executives have been found to manage their earnings aggressively, not only through accounting sleight-of-hand but also by skewing corporate policies in the hope of improving their company's apparent performance.

Earnings management in the present competitive world is an economic reality. Therefore, forensic accounting is now increasingly cracking down hard on people and their behavioural patterns who run these companies indulging in earnings management and questioning the efficacy of even those accounting procedures that were quite acceptable till a few years ago. The managers are dynamic and more learned today, and "so is easier to hide uncanny numbers under headings that are already fuzzy."

1.5.4 Regulation at crossroads

Global meltdown of 2007–08 is still fresh in the minds of corporate for two reasons: (i) it once again highlighted the need for an efficient corporate governance system worldwide and (ii) it was the focal point of struggling global markets. The Eurozone crisis of 2012 was the last straw on the camel's back, denting the confidence of global investors. The financial crisis and the resulting unsustainable levels of fiascos have undermined the world economy more seriously than anticipated. The real return has gone down. The business environment is more cautious and conservative in terms of cost-benefit trade-off due to rising incidents of fraud despite increasing regulation.

The world economy is at a crossroads. Silicon Valley Bank reinforced a question mark on the integrity of the governance system of the world's superpower. What can be said about other countries then? The investor base in the Indian corporate market largely consists of the promoter shareholders, their respective family members, and the government. The Companies Act, 2013 and SEBI (LODR) Regulations, 2015 added other feathers to this cap as an outcome of these past incidents.

Thus, to make the enterprises realise the importance of quality earnings and expect them to be profitably ethical, there is a serious requirement for determined and valiant efforts by way of forensic accounting. This would not only help shareholders' wealth maximisation but also resource allocation in general.

Reference

1. Popoola, O. M. J., Che-Ahmad, A. B. & Samsudin, R. S. 2015. An empirical investigation of fraud risk assessment and knowledge requirement on fraud related problem representation in Nigeria. *Accounting Research Journal*, 28, pp. 78–97.

2

FINANCIAL SHENANIGANS/ EARNINGS MANAGEMENT

Concept, motives and practices

The Satyam story, the Enron scandal, and numerous others show that a company's stated profits aren't always a reliable indicator of the state of its earnings. For starters, when calculating earnings and other financial measures, an accountant can choose from a variety of methods under "generally accepted accounting principles" (GAAP). Depending on the accounting method chosen, this could result in lower-quality financial information; that is how businesses manage earnings. This chapter explains the various facets of earnings management (EM): what earnings management is, why firms manage earnings, how firms manage earnings, and when they are most likely to do so. It arguably helps investors in assessing the reliability of companies' financial statements when they consider investment opportunities. Regulators and auditors may find it helpful to have a better understanding of managers' reasons for using earnings management when attempting to curb opportunistic behaviour.

DOI: 10.4324/9781003730187-2

2.1 What is financial shenanigan or earnings management?*

"Financial shenanigans" are actions that are taken to intentionally distort a company's reported financial performance. This manipulation is carried out with the help of accrual accounting. Financial shenanigans are exercised in the name of accounting flexibility, but their misuse is far from known, which ultimately erodes shareholders' value. Therefore, shareholders' wealth erosion becomes a major issue in light of growing corporate frauds worldwide.[1]

Financial shenanigans are often used interchangeably with "earnings management." (Earnings management and financial shenanigans both mean designing earnings.) Thus, "earnings management" is a strategy used by the management of a company to deliberately manipulate the companys' earnings so the figures match a predetermined target.

> Earnings management occurs when managers use judgment in financial reporting and in structuring transactions to alter financial reports to either mislead some stakeholders about the underlying economic performance of the company or to influence contractual outcomes that depend on reported accounting numbers undertakings.[2]

This definition captures both the "costly contracting approach" (earnings management is used to influence contractual outcomes) and the "informational approach" (earnings management is used to mislead stakeholders).

Earnings management does not always entail upward manipulation. As this will be shown, there are numerous situations in which managers purposefully understate corporate earnings. This is particularly likely to occur when businesses are

* Financial shenanigans or earnings management are also referred to as "creative accounting," i.e., creating numbers for a pre-determined objective by the management.

significantly above or below their goals. As stated by Michael Jensen:

> Earnings management has been considered an integral part of every top manager's job. But when managers smooth earnings to meet market projections, they're not creating value for the firm; they're both lying and making poor decisions that destroy value.[3]

Earnings management also does not have to be illegal. In most cases, what managers are doing is completely legal. They are using the discretion at their disposal to present their financial results in a manner that best suits their interests. Generally, it is the more aggressively optimistic outcomes that have been of concern to auditors and regulators.

2.2 Motives of financial shenanigans or earnings management

There are manifold reasons why managers manage earnings. Fundamentally, the reasons have to do with how well the company performs in comparison to a benchmark. The performance from the prior period (the aim to demonstrate an improving trend), analysts' expectations (the aim to meet or surpass expectations), "zero" (the aim to maintain profitability), or any other benchmark mentioned in a manager's compensation contract (the aim to reach a bonus threshold) could serve as this yardstick. Missing these benchmarks can be very expensive because of the highly non-linear relationship between stock price (or compensation) and earnings around the benchmarks.

So, financial shenanigans may be undertaken by entities with a view to managing impressions of the entity and may manifest in terms of the extremities of either conservatism or optimism. There are four basic incentives for these shenanigans:

1. Debt contracts
2. Compensation agreements

3. Equity offerings/analysts' forecasts
4. Insider trading

2.2.1 Debt contracts

Debt contracts are a major topic in financial shenanigans since lenders regularly use accounting data to evaluate business operations. One example of this theme is the imposition of performance limits on financing and investing activities. The rationale behind this incentive is that managers are encouraged to increase profits to avoid the costs of covenant violations or to lessen the burdensomeness of accounting-based restrictions in debt agreements.

Contracts between the business and its lending stakeholders are monitored and regulated with the use of accounting data. Lending contracts may offer incentives for earnings management since they are typically designed to stop managers from taking actions that benefit the company's stockholders at the expense of its creditors. Therefore, management information is communicated to stock investors, debt investors, and investors' representatives on boards of directors through financial reporting.

Due to asymmetric information on account of management knowingly not wanting to share, earnings manipulation is justified and may continue. The reason for the persistence is that managers would not like to communicate all of their internal information unless the principal has made a contractual commitment to share it. Such communication clauses create incentives for managers to divulge their inside information, which is crucial for managing earnings. Thus, earnings manipulation takes place as a part of a feasible reporting set within a given set of debt restrictions. These reporting frameworks evolve with the environment, which eventually results in various forms of earnings management. *For instance,* there is a strong incentive for managers to manage the accounting data used in debt agreements. The lenders' targets consequently result in an internal or stewardship incentive for managing earnings.

2.2.2 Compensation agreement

The literature suggests that managers are more likely to alter reported earnings to increase compensation. There is a significant relationship between earnings and their perks and monetary benefits. Overall, research findings support managers' use of accounting discretion to boost earnings-based bonus payments. Businesses with bonus award caps, for instance, are more likely than those with comparable performance but no bonus cap to report accruals that defer income when the cap is reached.

Financial shenanigans may originate as a result of meeting covenants of implicit compensation contracts.

1. When the earnings target in their bonus plan is not reached and they are eligible for the maximum bonuses allowed by the plan, divisional managers of a large multinational corporation are likely to postpone income.
2. In comparison to companies with comparable performance but no bonus cap, those with bonus caps are more likely to report accruals that defer income when the cap is reached. Firms with caps on bonuses are more likely to report accruals that defer income when that cap is reached than firms that have comparable performance but no bonus cap.

There are instances when there is an increase in the frequency of earnings management in periods when top managers' job security is threatened, or their expected tenure with the firm is short. During a proxy contest, incumbent managers exercise accounting discretion to boost reported earnings. Their short employment horizons and the short duration of their compensation contracts are also key factors in these manipulations.

2.2.3 Equity offerings/analysts' forecasts

Researchers have also looked at the importance of earnings management in the context of experienced equity offerings and initial public offerings. There is a correlation between return performance and subsequent earnings, which is relevant to the issue of earnings management.

Managers may feel pressure to manipulate earnings in an attempt to influence the stock price's performance in the near future because investors and financial analysts regularly use accounting data to help value stocks. These include accounting discretionary decisions made during capital market transactions and when the performance of the company differs from the expectations of analysts or investors.

Financial designing is driven by the expectations of management or financial analysts, as evidenced by public earnings forecasts. Indeed, it has been demonstrated that (i) managers take steps to control earnings upward in order to prevent reporting earnings below analyst forecasts, and (ii) financial analysts' stock recommendations (such as buy, hold, and sell) are a reliable indicator of financial manipulations, (iii) companies with a high percentage of growth prospects usually do not reduce research and development spending to prevent a decline in reported earnings, and (iv) companies falling short of management earnings forecasts use unexpected accruals to manage earnings upward.

2.2.4 Insider trading

In exchange for this invaluable service, managers who promptly gave investors insider (private) information were found to be able to act as knowledgeable traders by buying and selling stock before prices increased.

Earnings management may also be of interest to the managerial executives for antitrust reasons. It is often alleged that managers of firms vulnerable to fewer checks and balances and investigations have incentives to manage earnings to enjoy at others' cost.

2.3 Financial shenanigans' types and practices

Abuses in financial reporting have raised a red flag on the efficacy of the audit process and auditors' objectivity in certifying the credibility of their clients' earnings statements. The pervasive practice of "earnings management" is threatening the very integrity of financial reporting.

Typical accounting fraudulent practices could be categorised as:

1. Recognising revenue on false grounds
2. "Channel stuffing" to create the appearance of sales growth
3. "Secret" reserves
4. Capitalisation of expenses
5. Off-balance sheet items

2.3.1 Recognising false revenue

Businesses today work in incredibly stressful environments where investors won't overlook a company's inability to meet goals. Many institutions have been pressured to engage in revenue manipulation activities because they fear they won't be able to meet market expectations.

In this context, earnings-manipulation tactics can vary from slightly postponing the year-end shipping date to participating in false financial reporting through the use of fictitious sales figures.

When a company purposefully falsifies its financial records to create the appearance of controlled or disciplined growth, that is the full manifestation of fraudulent earnings management. Another tactic to boost revenue is to attract book customers. By using this stuffing, a company charges the seller for all related costs while billing the paper customer and holding the materials on their behalf. All of these strategies result in higher earnings during accounting periods.

Therefore, whether they are responding to market demands or are in dire need of funding, it is common for businesses to record revenue faster in order to present a positive picture of their operating outcomes.

There are various forms of earnings management (fraudulent) transactions practised by business firms under the above "sales premise." They are discussed as follows:

1. **Side agreements** – Sales terms and conditions may be modified or otherwise amended, which may impact revenue recognition. Common terms modifications may include the granting of rights of return, payment terms, exchange, or refunds. In the regular course of business, amendments to sales agreements are frequently and lawfully permitted. As long as revenue is recorded in the correct accounting period and suitable reserves are set up, there is nothing wrong with granting buyers the right of return or exchange.
2. **"Roundtrip" transactions** – Recording business transactions between two or more companies that don't seem to have any clear business sense, goal, or financial gain. These deals are frequently made in order to show rapid sales growth or inflate revenues. A loan to a customer or an investment in a customer to buy the goods are examples of such transactions, as are sales between businesses for the same amount. Even though money may be exchanged, if there is no underlying business goal or financial gain for the transaction, payment by itself does not validate the transaction or support the recognition of revenue.
3. **Alteration of shipping documents** – An organisation may record false sales transactions and recognise improper revenue by creating false shipping documents. By altering the shipping dates and terms of shipping documents, a company may increase its revenue shown in a specific accounting period.
4. **Up-front fees** – In certain sales transactions, clients must pay upfront fees for services that will be rendered over a long period of time. Before the services are rendered and thus before revenue is generated, organisations might try to recognise the entire contract amount. Financial documents like purchase orders, sales invoices, and sales contracts may be altered as part of such schemes.

2.3.2 Channel stuffing

When a business purposefully manipulates its accounting to give the impression of controlled or disciplined growth, earnings management is fully realised. Another tactic to boost sales is to provide customers with financial incentives, such as price breaks, extended payment terms, or other concessions, to encourage them to write purchase orders well in advance of their needs. This is called "channel stuffing."

BILL AND HOLD

"Bill and hold" is a popular variation of channel stuffing. When products are booked as sales but delivery and ownership transfer do not take place on the day the organisation records the sale, this is known as a bill and hold transaction. Although purchase orders or sales orders may be legitimately issued in these kinds of transactions, the customer may not be able or willing to accept the product's delivery at the time the sale is recorded. The contract may state that the buyer may return any items if they are not sold and that the seller is responsible for paying for all shipping costs (both ways) and storage costs. All of these financial costs result in lower profits and weaker sales.

2.3.3 Secret reserves

Accounting frauds can be committed by smoothing earnings to help maintain the firm's earnings streams ex-ante or by manipulating earnings upward to achieve ex-post earnings rises. In the fine print of delicate and arbitrary accounting estimations, such as reserves and provisions in the profit and loss and balance sheet, such deception of earnings takes place. One of the smoothing methods is the ad hoc creation or revocation of the accounting estimate for the discretionary debt reserve.

Therefore, for all market participants to make better financial decisions, they must have an understanding of how managers can create these hidden items. According to *The Economist* (2010),[4] Dell was discovered by the Securities and Exchange

Commission (SEC) to be keeping "cookie-jar reserves" with funds from Intel. As per the SEC, Dell would have failed to meet the experts' earnings projections for each quarter from 2002 to 2006. One such agreement was with the large semiconductor manufacturer Intel. As per the agreement, Dell was required to exclusively utilise Intel's central processing unit chips in its computers; the payments for these chips were kept confidential. As a result, Dell faces a $100 million fine.[4]

2.3.4 Expense capitalisation

Another common method of accounting fraud is inaccurately treating revenue expenses as capital expenses and presenting them as fixed assets on the balance sheet. In financial statements, the management may decide to show charges for R&D and other ancillary expenses as assets rather than expenses. This ultimately leads to an increase in the company's net worth.

Contrary to the accounting nature of items, this is a very common practice. A business owner typically believes that the expenses of the company are his own when he treats them as capital items for various benefits. Usually, these business strategies are deliberately disregarded in financial reporting.

2.3.5 Off-balance sheet items

Financial commitments and assurances made on behalf of subsidiary companies are frequently concealed by classifying the transactions as "contingent liabilities" and excluding them from the primary balance sheet.

The aforementioned strategy has an effect on thresholders' ability to generate long-term wealth, which erodes the company's profits. Therefore, everyone involved in the market needs to understand how managers can manipulate earnings in order to make better financial decisions. By understanding the tactics managers use, market participants can lessen the effects of manipulation and eventually decrease the effectiveness of earnings management techniques. Scholars and financial experts are unquestionably significant in this regard.

References

1. Goel, Sandeep. 2013. Decoding Gimmicks of Financial Shenanigans in Telecom Sector in India. *Journal of Accounting and Management Information Systems*, 12(1), pp. 118–131. http://online-cig.ase.ro/jcig/art/paper_1842.pdf
2. Healey, P. M. & Wahlen, J. M. 1999. A review of the earnings management literature and its implications for Standard Setting. *Accounting Horizons*, 4(368), p. 13,365.
3. Jensen, M. 2004. *Agency costs of overvalued equity.* Harvard NOM Research Paper No. 04-26, 12 pages.
4. The Economist. 2010. *Taking away Dell's cookie jar* [Online]. Available at: http://www.economist.com/blogs/newsbook/2010/07/dells_sec_settlement (accessed on 24 October 2016).

3

FORENSIC ANALYTICS

Tools and techniques

The issue of measuring the effects of managers' use of accounting discretion in the form of accounting models or method choices is inevitable in fraud detection. Different frauds require a new approach to test for financial shenanigans, but the premise of earnings manipulation is more or less common. These techniques examine the distribution of reported earnings to assess whether there is any evidence of earnings management and hypothesise that corporate managers have incentives to avoid reporting losses or reporting declines in earnings and examine the distribution of reported earnings around these points. The findings indicate that there is a higher-than-expected frequency of firms with slightly positive earnings and a lower-than-expected frequency of firms with slightly negative earnings. Forensic accountants employ a wide range of techniques and tools to uncover fraud and financial irregularities. These methods help them analyse financial data, identify patterns, and detect anomalies.

3.1 Accruals management: Financial shenanigan premise!

This section demystifies accruals management misuse for financial shenanigans.

DOI: 10.4324/9781003730187-3

Basically, the operational definition of financial shenanigans or earnings management (EM) is the potential use of "accrual management" with the objective of obtaining some personal gain.

> The following accrual relationship is central to an understanding of EM:
>
> Total accruals = Nondiscretionary accruals + Discretionary accruals

A. The foundation of accrual accounting is the notion that costs and expenses differ from benefits and revenue. Due to this, net income can be thought of as the operational cash flow adjusted for temporary components, which yields net income from operations.

   "Accruals" are adjustment items. The distribution of revenue and expenses over time involves several subjective choices. The accruals are subject to greater discretion than cash flows and show a company's accounting decisions.

B. Total accruals in forensic analysis for investigating financial manipulations are typically separated into *(i) discretionary and (ii) non-discretionary accruals.*

   Non-discretionary accruals are required by business activities.

   Non-discretionary accruals are a function of revenues. For example, revenue growth usually increases accounts receivable or inventory.

   Similarly, non-discretionary accruals are a function of investment in gross property, plant, and equipment, because these investments usually increase depreciation.

   Discretionary accruals consist of accruals that are not required by activities and are indexed to companies' total assets or sales.

> "**Discretionary accruals**" are the portion of accruals that are subject to managerial discretion and are often used as a "proxy" for financial shenanigans or earnings management.
>
> *Yearly trends in these indices are considered as the indicators of the manipulation.*

- Discretionary accruals are not closely related to the economic circumstances of the firm. Discretionary accruals can be observed by the amount the actual accruals deviate from the non-discretionary accruals level.
- The general approach for estimating discretionary accruals is to regress total accruals on variables that are proxies for normal accruals. The unexplained (residual) components of total accruals are referred to as unexpected accruals or discretionary accruals.
- Broadly, the discretionary line of items is classified into three types, which are often used and have a high impact on the reported earnings:
  - Accounting changes (in policies and methods)
  - Extraordinary items (not arising in the normal course of business – unusual or infrequent)
  - Restructuring provisions (disposal or reorganisation charges).

3.2 Tools and techniques of fraud analysis

Various tools and techniques developed and are used specifically for decoding financial shenanigans as part of the forensic accounting investigation, and process are explained as follows:

3.2.1 The quality metrics

- "Quality of earnings" is an important determinant in determining earnings manipulation. It can be found by computing the percentage of operating cash flows to net income of a firm. Higher the quality of earnings, the lower the chances of earnings manipulation. Cash flow from operations should be positive and larger than net income; if not, the reasons need to be investigated. The minimum expected level of quality of earnings is about one, or 100%, and higher than this is always better. This is really an important indication to analysts and investors of the problems going on with the company.[1]

- "Quality of revenue" is another important determinant in determining earnings manipulation. It can be found out by computing the percentage of collection of sales in cash. Higher the quality of revenue, the lesser the chances of earnings manipulation. Company analysts closely look at the quality of revenue, as well as the quality of earnings.[2]

3.2.2 *The total accruals model – discretionary*

The discretionary portion of accruals is the difference between total accruals in the event year t scaled by total assets (A_t–1) and nondiscretionary accruals (NDA_t). The measure of nondiscretionary accruals (NDA_t) rests on last period's total accruals (TA_t–1).

Thus, discretionary accruals (DAC_{it}) are:

$$DAC_{it} = \frac{(TA_{it} - TA_{it-1})}{A_{it-1}}$$

Note: TA_{it} and A_{it}–1 are total accruals and total assets for period t and t–1 for firm i.

For the computation of accruals, two methods are generally used: the balance sheet approach and the cash-flow approach.

(a) *The balance sheet approach*

The balance sheet approach for the computation of total accruals (TA) is as follows:

$$TA_t = \Delta CA_t - \Delta Cash_t - \Delta CL_t + \Delta DCL_t - DEP_t$$

where,
ΔCA_t is the change in the current assets in year t;
$\Delta Cash_t$ is the change in cash and cash equivalents in year t;
ΔCL_t is the change in current liabilities in the year t;
ΔDCL_t is the change in debt included in current liabilities in the year t; and
DEP_t is the depreciation and amortisation expense in the year.

(b) *The cash-flow approach*

The traditional balance sheet approach to the measurement of total accruals suffers from potential contamination of the estimation error. To overcome this problem, an alternative method is recommended to measure accruals.

This approach calculates accruals directly from the cash flow statement as follows:

$$TA_{cf} = NI - CFO_{cf}$$

where,
TA_{cf} is the total accrual adjustments provided on the cash flow statement under the indirect method;
NI is the net earnings of the business; and
CFO_{cf} is the cash flows from operations/operating cash flows (from continuing operations) taken directly from the cash flow statement.

3.2.3 The Beneish profit model

Financial reporting leads to financial analysis by stakeholders and the differentiation of high- and low-performing firms. Therefore, managers use their judgement when it comes to financial reporting and open the door for "financial shenanigans" to represent the company's desired financial situation.

In this context, the use of a profit model that can yield an earnings manipulation index is desired. "Beneish profit model"[3] applies a linear combination of financial variables to be converted to a "profitability manipulation."

Beneish uses a number of variables to proxy for the "probability of manipulation" that the market will detect through financial statement distortions. This distinguishes between GAAP violators and control firms.

The five financial statement variables* designed to capture distortions in financial statement data to assess the probability of detection are:

1. *Day's sales in receivables index* – measuring whether changes in receivables are in time with changes in sales.
2. *Gross margin index* – analysing whether gross margins have deteriorated, a negative signal about a firm's prospects.
3. *Asset quality index* – assessing shifts in the risk of asset realisation, where an increase is seen as a sign of a greater inclination to capitalise and defer costs.
4. *Sales growth index* – examining growth in sales with respect to the previous year to find out whether the company is adding fake sales.
5. *Total accruals to total assets* – determining the extent to which earnings are cash-based, with high increases in non-cash working capital to reflect possible manipulation.

These variables are explained below:

1 Day's sales in receivables index (DSRI)

$$\text{DSRI}=\frac{\text{Receivables}_t/\text{Sales}_t}{\text{Receivables}_{t-1}/\text{Sales}_{t-1}}$$

* A common approach is to use a five-variable model. However, an eight-variable model is also available in the literature. *The eight-variable Beneish M-Score expands upon the five-variable model by incorporating additional financial variables (DEPI, SGAI, and LVGI).*

DSRI is the ratio of days sales in receivables in the first year (year t) to the corresponding measure in year t–1. This shows the change in receivables at time t by comparing them at time t–1 according to sales. This index is anticipated to have a linear structure as long as the company's credit sales policy does not undergo significant changes.

A large increase in days' sales in receivables could be the result of a change in credit policy to boost sales due to heightened competition, but disproportionate increases in receivables relative to sales could also suggest revenue inflation. Thus, a material increase in the index indicates a higher probability that the companys' receivables are manipulative.

2 Gross margin index (GMI)

$$\text{GMI}=\frac{\left(\text{Sales}_{t-1}\text{-Cost of Goods Sold}_{t-1}\right)/\text{Sales}_{t-1}}{\left(\text{Sales}_{t}\text{-Cost of Gods Sold}_{t}\right)/\text{Sales}_{t}}$$

GMI is the ratio of the gross margin in year t–1 to the gross margin in year t. If GMI is greater than 1, it indicates that the gross margin of the company has deteriorated. Gross margin deterioration is a negative signal about firms' prospects. Firms with poorer prospects (with weaker profitability) are more likely to engage in earnings manipulation – to create artificial profits or decrease losses.

It fundamentally alerts you that the risk of earnings manipulation is higher when gross margins drop. But, if the company is already inflating earnings, gross margins will be just the opposite: higher than normal.

3 Asset quality index (AQI)

$$\text{AQI}=\frac{\dfrac{1\text{-}\left(\text{Current assets}_{t}\text{+Net fixed assets}_{t}\right)}{\text{Total Assets}_{t}}}{\dfrac{1\text{-}\left(\text{Current assets}_{t-1}\text{+Net fixed assets}_{t-1}\right)}{\text{Total Assets}_{t-1}}}$$

Asset quality in a given year is the ratio of non-current assets (other than property, plant, and equipment (PPE)) to total assets and measures the percentage of total assets for which future benefits may be less certain. AQI shows the change in other non-current assets within total assets relative to the previous year.

AQI is the ratio of asset quality in year t, as compared to asset quality in year t–1. If the index is greater than 1, it is an indicator that the company will capitalise its expenses instead of writing them as current period expenses on the income statement. In other words, it indicates increased efforts on the part of the company to defer costs. This situation is considered manipulation of financial information.

4 Sales growth index (SGI)

$$SGI = \frac{Sales_t}{Sales_{t-1}}$$

SGI is the ratio of sales in year t to sales in year t–1. Sales growth does not necessarily imply the manipulation of financial datasets; however, professionals believe that growth firms are more likely to commit financial statement fraud because managers are under pressure to meet earnings targets due to their financial position and capital needs.

An increase in the index reflects a rise in sales, which may or may not be legitimate.

5 Total accruals to total assets (TATA)

$$TATA = \frac{\Delta \text{Working capital} - \Delta \text{Cash - Depreciation } t}{\text{Total Assets } t}$$

Total accruals are calculated as the change in working capital accounts (other than cash) less depreciation.

"Total accruals to total assets" is used as a proxy for the amount of cash that supports reported earnings, and expects higher positive accruals (less cash) to be linked with a higher likelihood of earnings manipulation. An increase in accruals from one period to the next may indicate management is manipulating earnings through its discretionary control over accrual policy.

In this context, if non-cash working capital increases or decreases dramatically, it is assumed that manipulation of financial information takes place. So, it indicates the volume of earnings that result from accruals rather than cash flows.

The earnings manipulation index, proposed by Beneish probit analysis, is expressed as the following linear combination:

$$\text{Manipulation Index } (P) = -6.065 + 0.823 * (DSRI) + 0.906 * (GMI) + 0.593 * (AQI) + 0.717 * (SGI) + 0.107 * (TATA)$$

The probability of manipulation is denoted by *P – the M-Score.*

In essence, when interpreting the M-Score, follow these guidelines:

1. **Likely Manipulator:** An M-Score **greater than –1.78** suggests that the company is likely engaging in earnings manipulation.
2. **Possible Manipulator:** An M-Score **between –2.22 and –1.78** indicates a possible risk of manipulation, warranting further investigation.
3. **Unlikely Manipulator:** An M-Score **less than –2.22** implies that the company is unlikely to be manipulating its earnings.

3.2.4 The Altman Z score

The Altman Z-score model is a measure of a company's financial strength that uses a weighted sum of several factors. It is used as a 'Predictor of bankruptcy,' a numerical metric that is used to forecast a company's likelihood of getting bankrupt within the next two years. The model was developed by Edward Altman, an American professor of finance in 1968 as a measure of businesses' financial stability at the time of the Great Depression, when businesses experienced a sharp rise in incidences of default.

It is considered an effective method of predicting the state of financial distress of any organisation by using multiple income statement and balance sheet values. The Z-score model is based on five key financial ratios. *In addition to financial ratios that forecast a company's likelihood of going bankrupt, Altman score employs a weighting system for using the model.*

Altman's Z-Score Model Formula

$$Z = 1.2X1 + 1.4X2 + 3.3X3 + 0.6X4 + 1.0X5$$

where:

Z is the Altman's Z score

X1 is the Working Capital/Total Assets ratio

X2 is the Retained Earnings/Total Assets ratio

X3 is the Earnings Before Interest and Tax (EBIT)/Total Assets ratio

X4 is the Market Value of Equity/Total Liabilities ratio

X5 is the Sales/Total Assets ratio

1 Working capital/total assets

Working capital is the difference between the current assets of a company and its current liabilities. The value of a company's working capital determines its short-term financial health. A positive working capital means that a company can meet its short-term financial obligations and have adequate funds available to invest and grow.

In contrast, negative working capital means that a company will struggle to meet its short-term financial obligations because there are inadequate current assets.

2 Retained earnings/total assets

The retained earnings/total assets ratio shows the amount of retained earnings or losses in a company. If a company reports a low retained earnings to total assets ratio, it means that it is financing its expenditure using borrowed funds rather than funds from its reserves and surplus. It increases the probability of a company going bankrupt.

On the other hand, a high retained earnings to total assets ratio shows that a company uses its retained earnings to fund capital expenditures. It shows that the company achieved profitability over the years, and it does not need to rely on borrowings.

3 EBIT/Total assets

EBIT as a measure of a company's profitability refers to the ability of a company to generate profits mainly from its core operations. The EBIT/Total Assets ratio demonstrates a company's ability to generate enough revenues to stay profitable, fund ongoing operations, and make debt payments.

4 Market value of equity/total liabilities

The market value of equity, also known as market capitalisation of a company, is obtained by multiplying the number of outstanding shares by the current price of stocks.

The market value of the equity/total liabilities ratio shows the degree to which a company's market value would decline when it declares bankruptcy before the value of liabilities exceeds the value of assets on the balance sheet. A high market value of equity to total liabilities ratio can be interpreted to mean high investor confidence in the company's financial strength.

5 Sales/total assets

The sales to total assets ratio shows how efficiently the management utilises its assets to generate sales vis-à-vis the competition. A high sales to total assets ratio means that the management requires a small investment to generate sales, which increases the overall profitability of the company.

In contrast, a low or falling sales to total assets ratio means that the management will need to use more resources to generate enough sales, which will reduce the company's profitability.

WHAT DOES Z-SCORE MEAN?

It indicates whether the probability of bankruptcy is high or low. Bankruptcy increases with a lower Z score.

- *Z score of 3 or higher:* The business is 'safe' and unlikely to declare bankruptcy.
- *Z score between 1.8 and 3:* A company is in the "gray" area and has a moderate chance of declaring bankruptcy.
- *Z score less than 1.8:* A company is in 'financial distress' and has a high likelihood of going bankrupt.

The above scales are presented in Figure 3.1.

Using Altman's Z score, investors can decide whether to purchase or sell a company's stock based on its evaluated financial

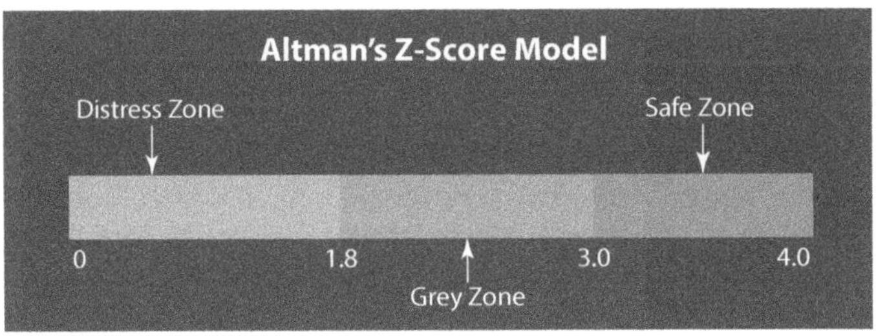

FIGURE 3.1 Altman Z-score metric

strength. Since there is little chance that a company will go bankrupt in the near future, investors may decide on buying the company's stock if its Z score is closer to 3. However, if it displays a Z score closer to 1.8, the investors may think about selling the company's stock in order to protect their capital.

Altman score example!

Altman score example!

Suppose a public manufacturing company ABC Ltd. is at risk of insolvency following several periods of declining profitability and losses being incurred.

Using the Z-score model, we'll estimate the chance of bankruptcy of ABC Ltd.

Financials:

- Current Assets = \$60 million
- Current Liabilities = \$40 million
- Fixed Assets = \$100 million
- Net Income/PAT = \$10 million
- Dividend = \$2 million
- Sales = \$60 million
- COGS and SG&A = \$40 million
- P/E Multiple = 8.0x
- Total Liabilities = \$120 million

Solution:

I. Calculation of indicators:

- Working Capital = \$60 million – \$40 million = \$20 million
- Total Assets = \$60 million + \$100 million = \$160 million
- Retained Earnings = \$10 million – \$2 million = \$8 million
- Operating Income (EBIT) = \$60 million – \$40 million = \$20 million
- Market Capitalisation = 8.0x × \$10 million = \$80 million

It can be observed that the company's net profit margin (PAT/sale) is approximately 17%, with a dividend payout ratio (dividend/PAT) of 20%. It is not really encouraging. If necessary, those dividend payments would need to be checked soon. Further, the P/E multiple is low.

II. Calculation of ratios:

- X1 = Working Capital ÷ Total Assets = 0.13
- X2 = Retained Earnings ÷ Total Assets = 0.05
- X3 = EBIT ÷ Total Assets = 0.13
- X4 = Market Capitalisation ÷ Total Liabilities = 0.67
- X5 = Sales ÷ Total Assets = 0.38

III. Altman Z score:

TABLE 3.1 Z Score calculation

	Ratios	*Weightage*	*Z Score*
Working Capital/Total Assets	0.13	1.20	0.16
Etained Earnings/Total Assets	0.05	1.40	0.07
EBIT/Total Assets	0.13	3.30	0.43
Market Value of Equity/ Total Liabilities	0.67	0.60	0.40
Sales/Total Assets	0.38	1.00	0.38
			1.44

Note: This implied zone is Distress.

Since the Z score of 1.40 is below 1.8, the company is in the "Distress Zone," where the risk of near-term insolvency is high.

3.2.5 The Benford's law

Benford's law describes the relative frequency distribution of a dataset's leading digits. Smaller leading digit values are more common than larger ones. If all digits were represented equally, then they would each appear one-ninth (about 11.1%) of the time.

Yet in an uncanny number of real-world data sets, an astonishing 30.1% of the entries begin with a 1, 17.6% begin with a 2, and so on. This phenomenon is known as *Benford's law.*

According to this law, approximately 30% of numbers start with a 1 while less than 5% start with a 9. This law states that leading 1s occur 6.5 times more frequently than leading 9s! Benford's law is also known as the "First Digit Law."

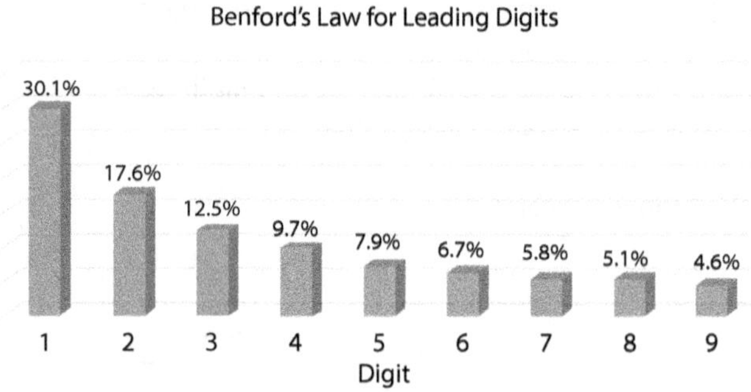

FIGURE 3.2 Benford's law of digitisation

Figure 3.2 displays the distribution of leading digits according to Benford's law.

The leading digits of population, stock prices, sports statistics, social media likes, billing amounts, and financial and tax data, for instance, frequently follow this distribution.

Use of Benford's law

It has been widely used by analysts to look for "fraud" and "manipulation" in financial records, tax returns, applications, and decision-making documents. They use Benford's law to compare the leading digit distribution in these datasets. *When the leading digits don't follow the distribution, it's a red flag for fraud in some datasets.*

There is a simple explanation for why this works. When people manipulate numbers, they don't track the frequencies of their fake leading digits, producing an unnatural distribution of leading digits. In some cases, they might systematically adjust the leading digits to be below a particular threshold value. For example, if the transaction type has a $100,000 limit, fraudsters might start many numbers with a 9 for $99,000.

> "Using Benford's law to find fraud is admissible in local, state, and federal US courts." Using Benford's law to find fraud is admissible in local, state, and federal US courts. In the past, it has detected irregularities in Greece's EU application and investment return data for Ponzi schemes, such as Bernie Madoff's.**

It works best for data that ranges over multiple orders of magnitudes from extremely low to extremely high. You can cover the 10s, 100s, 1000s, and so on. For instance, population and incomes can vary greatly. *If a dataset that you would expect to follow Benford's curve doesn't, it's just a red flag and not evidence of fraud. However, the auditors and investigators can target dubious records more effectively.*

Benford's law formula:

$$P(d) = \log_{10}\left(1 + \frac{1}{d}\right)$$

where d = the values of the leading digits from 1 to 9.

The formula calculates the probability for each leading digit.

Table 3.2 displays the probabilities that Benford's law formula calculates for all digits.

** https://statisticsbyjim.com/probability/benfords-law. Jim Frost.

TABLE 3.2 Benford's probability score

First digit	*Benford Per Cent of Occurrence as First Digit*
1	30.10%
2	17.61%
3	12.49%
4	9.69%
5	7.92%
6	6.69%
7	5.80%
8	5.12%
9	4.58%

In general, Benford's law applies to data that meet the following criteria:

- *Quantitative data*
- *Larger datasets*
- *Multiple magnitudes, from very low to very high*
- *No restriction of minimums or maximums*
- *Measurable data*

It doesn't apply to assigned data (numbers), such as phone numbers/ID numbers, etc.

Example!

Let's take an empirical example of Benford's law using "Excel."

- We downloaded the sales of a manufacturing sector company Gen Ltd. in India for 2023–24. Do the leading digits for these sales numbers follow the hypothesised distribution?
- The dataset satisfies the above assumption – multiple orders of magnitudes from extremely low 85 to extremely 98,657 high (in INR). The large sample size (n = 1006). So, the data is theoretically perfect for this test.

- For using Excel, we need two Excel functions.
    - Left: To get the leading (or other) digit.
    - Countif: To get the counts for each leading digit.
- Figure 3.3 shows the results in graph format with Data Labels. On the chart, the 'Black' line represents the relative frequency of each leading digit observed in the dataset, while the 'Grey' line indicates the values that Benford's law predicts.

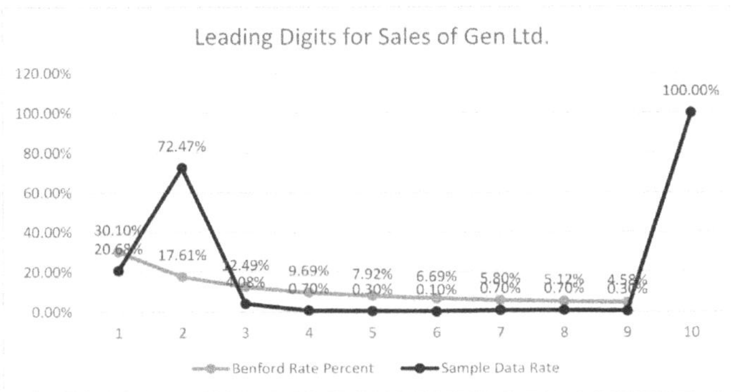

FIGURE 3.3 Benford's digitisation of "Sales" of Gen Ltd.

In summary, these tests provide convincing evidence that some firms do manage earnings when they anticipate reporting a loss, an earnings decline, or falling short of investors' expectations.

References

1. Goel, Sandeep. 2014. The quality of reported numbers by the management: A Case Testing of Earnings Management in Corporate India. *Journal of Financial Crime*, 21(3), pp. 355–376.
2. Goel, Sandeep. 2014. The quality of reported numbers by the management: A Case Testing of Earnings Management in Corporate India. *Journal of Financial Crime*, 21(3), pp. 355–376.
3. Beneish, M. D. 1997. Detecting GAAP violation: Implications for assessing earnings management among firms with extreme financial performance. *Journal of Accounting and Public Policy*, 16, pp. 271–309.

4

FINANCIAL SHENANIGANS ANALYSES AND DISCUSSION

This chapter reviews the magnitude and frequency of financial shenanigans of corporate enterprises in India and diagnoses their scale on the firm's earnings and the accounting choices of managers. It makes use of the published (secondary) data for the analyses of earnings hazards of the sample companies and presents the results for further detailed investigation. Various forensic accounting tools and techniques discussed in the previous chapter have been applied in the study. *This provides the necessary direction to carry out the study at the next level.*

4.1 Research design

The present study covers the listed companies in India.* Keeping in view the differences in the objectives and functions of these companies, the present research would concentrate only on the companies in the private sector.

The enterprises have been chosen on the basis of their performance in terms of profit generation (PAT performance) for the year 2023–24. The ten leading corporate enterprises were considered for the final discussion, on a selective basis. They happened to be from diverse sectors and their list is given in Appendix I. The period to be covered in the present research

* The names of companies are disguised for the discussion.

DOI: 10.4324/9781003730187-4

study would be five years, ranging from 2019–20 to 2023–24. It has been taken as it would be meaningful enough to focus the attention on earnings management practices of the enterprises chosen, detect the various grey areas, and reveal the short-term and long-term changes to permit the valid conclusions thereof.

The companies chosen with their sector and nature of business are mentioned as follows:

Company A – manufacturing (textile, petrochemicals)
Company B – manufacturing (metal and mining)
Company C – manufacturing (steel)
Company D – service (information technology)
Company E – service (information technology)
Company F – manufacturing (tobacco and fast-moving consumer goods)
Company G – manufacturing (aluminium)
Company H – manufacturing (heavy industry and construction)
Company I – manufacturing (automobile)
Company J – manufacturing (textile)

4.2 Earnings' quality

The quality of earnings (profits) in the sample companies was computed for the period 2019–20 to 2023–24. The quality of earnings is presented in Table 4.1 and Figure 4.1. The complete financial database, i.e., operating cash flow, net income, and quality of earnings in the units, is presented in Appendix I.

An examination of Table 4.1 and Appendix I shows a vast range of quality of earnings in the sample companies. There is a huge difference in the quality of earnings among the units under study. I Ltd. leads the sample units in earnings quality with an average of 168.35%, whereas E Ltd. has the lowest average of 84.70%.

Company A has an average earnings quality of 160.19%. It has been well above 100%, which is very encouraging. But on the other hand, the trend in the quality of their earnings over the years has been quite a decreasing trend. This is a concern.

TABLE 4.1 Quality of earnings for the sample companies, 2019–20 to 2023–24 (in %)

Company	*2019–20*	*2020–21*	*2021–22*	*2022–23*	*2023–24*
1. A Ltd.	228.24%	228.33%	113.59%	141.25%	89.56%
2. B Ltd.	122.19%	-326.94%	142.00%	-104.51%	89.89%
3. C Ltd.	166.90%	109.86%	103.57%	121.22%	133.44%
4. D Ltd.	131.40%	71.40%	92.40%	86.07%	85.37%
5. E Ltd.	99.89%	111.48%	94.64%	94.11%	23.37%
6. F Ltd.	118.86%	84.48%	86.33%	79.30%	87.27%
7. G Ltd.	132.71%	132.46%	42.89%	130.11%	74.79%
8. H Ltd.	62.02%	11.34%	135.28%	151.85%	89.50%
9. I Ltd.	335.36%	101.04%	-14.46%	115.50%	304.32%
10. J Ltd.	150.04%	118.60%	148.55%	112.82%	93.66%

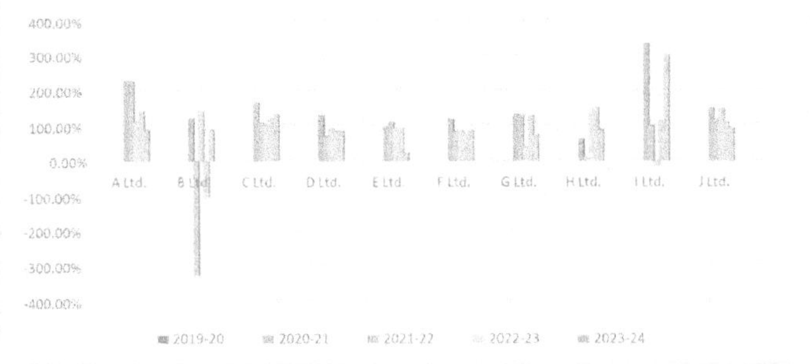

FIGURE 4.1 Earnings quality trend for the sample companies, 2019–20 to 2023–24

The management must check this trend to stop it from further decline. B Ltd. does not show very promising quality of earnings. It has an average of –15.47%, indicating negative quality of earnings. In 2020–21, there is a huge deficit between their earnings and the amount of cash actually generated by operating activities. In fact, cash flow from operations has been negative this year. A similar negative trend can be seen in 2022–23. In other years, its performance has been satisfactory. But overall, it requires constant efforts by the management. Company C also performs well with an average of 127.00%. Though their performance declined in 2020–21 and 2021–22, over the last two years, they have again shown an increasing trend in earnings quality.

In D Ltd., the level of earnings quality has been below 100%. They have an average of 93.33%. Moreover, their trend of earnings quality is also on quite a declining spree. This is alarming, and some serious efforts are really required by the management to improve this. E Ltd. has the lowest average of 84.70%, much below 100%. Their trend of earnings quality has also been declining over the years. In fact, last year, viz. 2023–24, was the worst year for the unit. This can be verified with their ratio of 23.37%. There is a huge gap between their earnings and the amount of cash actually generated by operating activities.

It requires serious concern from the management. F Ltd. more or less shows the same performance as the former two units. Its average quality of earnings is 91.25%. It is really showing a fluctuating quality trend over the years. This is not a healthy sign. Stability of earnings quality is very much required in the long run.

In case of G Ltd., the average quality of earnings has been above 100%, i.e. 102.50%. Both 2021–22 and the last year 2023–24 have been really bad for the company in terms of quality of earnings. In 2021–22, the ratio was 42.89% and last year it was 74.79%; very low compared to other years. In these years, operating cash flows have been quite low vis-à-vis total earnings. This trend should not continue further. H Ltd. shows an average quality of earnings below 100%, i.e. 90.00%. Its trend is also quite fluctuating during the period. This is not a good indicator for long-term growth. Company I has really shown a good quality of earnings during the period. It leads all the units with an average earnings quality of 168.35%. They have also experienced negative quality of earnings in 2021–22, but otherwise, their performance has been more than satisfactory. J Industries also performs quite well with an average of 124.73%. But one cause for concern is that their earnings quality has been on quite a declining trend during the period. This is not a healthy sign, and efforts are required to check this for future implications.

4.3 Quality of revenue

The quality of revenue (sales and services) in the sample companies were computed for period 2019–20 to 2023–24. The quality of revenue is presented in Table 4.2 and Figure 4.2 and complete financial database, i.e., cash collected, sales, and quality of revenue in the units, is presented in Appendix II.

An examination of Table 4.2 and Appendix II shows a serious requirement for quality of revenue in the sample companies. Except for C Ltd. and I Ltd., other units have shown poor quality of revenue during the period.

TABLE 4.2 Quality of revenue for the sample companies, 2019–20 to 2023–24 (in %)

Company	*2019–20*	*2020–21*	*2021–22*	*2022–23*	*2023–24*
1. A Ltd.	–0.09%	–1.01%	–0.26%	0.36%	–1.79%
2. B Ltd.	–4.01%	–2.45%	–2.10%	–2.72%	0.61%
3. C Ltd.	2.58%	0.44%	0.25%	–0.47%	0.40%
4. D Ltd.	–2.53%	-9.04%	–2.94%	–5.89%	-5.12%
5. E Ltd.	–5.20%	–4.77%	–5.66%	–4.49%	-6.24%
6. F Ltd.	–0.20%	–2.23%	–0.12%	–0.45%	–0.47%
7. G Ltd.	–0.01%	–2.16%	–3.70%	–1.29%	–0.29%
8. H Ltd.	–2.75%	–4.86%	–5.25%	–3.85%	–7.38%
9. I Ltd.	2.18%	–0.97%	0.35%	–0.21%	–1.06%
10. J Ltd.	–0.90%	–0.52%	1.43%	–1.70%	–1.17%

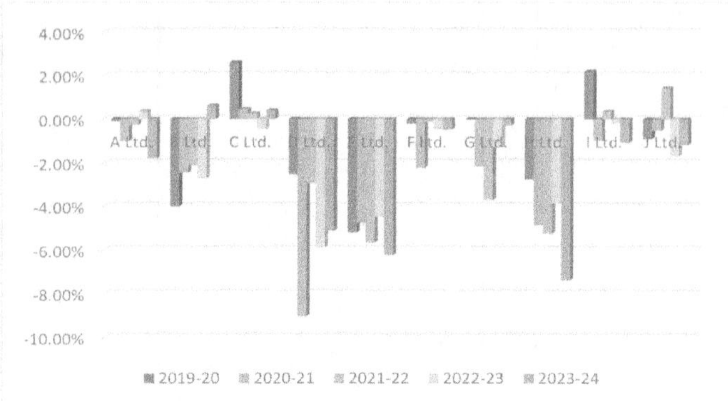

FIGURE 4.2 Revenue quality trend for the sample companies, 2019–20 to 2023–24

A Ltd. has shown an average collection of sales of –0.56% during the period. It is not a good sign. There is a huge gap between their sales and the amount of cash actually collected. In fact, except for 2022–23, there has not been collection of reported sales in all other years. It needs to be looked into by the management. B Ltd. goes a step further with an average of –2.13%. But there is one positive sign that their negative trend has been declining over the years, resulting in a positive ratio of 0.61% in the last year. C Ltd. shows a promising revenue quality picture with an average of 0.64%. But one cause for concern is the declining trend of revenue quality. It should be checked upon by the management.

D Ltd. also shows a poor performance with regard to revenue quality. They have an average of –5.10%. Also, they are experiencing quite a fluctuating trend of revenue quality. It is not a good sign. E Ltd. shows a similar trend to the former unit in the quality of earnings. They have an average quality of earnings of –5.27%. There has not been any collection of reported sales over the years. Company F also shows a negative average revenue quality though lower as compared to other units. They have an average of –0.70%. Their collection of reported sales has been zero during the period.

G Ltd. also has a negative average revenue quality of –1.49%. There is a huge deficit between sales and cash collected out of reported sales. The trend is also quite fluctuating, which is another reason to worry. In the case of H Ltd., the collection of sales over the years has been poor, and it is evident in their average of –4.82%. I Ltd. has a positive average revenue quality of 0.06%. But they have also undergone bad years, i.e., 2020–21, 2022–23, and 2023–24. There has been no collection of cash during these years. This should not continue in the future. J Industries shows a negative average revenue quality though lower as compared to other units. They have an average of –0.57%. They have reported a promising year as well in 2021–22. They have 1.43% collection of sales in the year. Overall, the quality of revenue in the sample companies is poor compared to the quality of earnings. So, efforts are required by the management of the sample companies to take a closer look at the quality of revenue to really improve it.

4.4 Discretionary accruals and earnings manipulation

Managers have the flexibility of selecting between the alternative ways to account for transactions as well as choosing between accrual options within the same accounting treatment. This flexibility can enable managers to adapt to economic circumstances and portray the correct economic consequences of transactions; it can also be used to influence the level of earnings at any particular time with the objective of securing gains for management and the stakeholders. This is the essence of earnings management, which is the ability to "manipulate" the choices available and make the discretionary choices that can achieve a desired level of income.

As discretionary accruals are a proxy for earnings management, their trend indicates income-accrual management exercised by a company. If the trend in accruals is negative (positive), it indicates managers are making income-decreasing (increasing) accrual decisions, for example more (less) depreciations or decrease (increase) in inventory.

The total accruals *(TACC)* and discretionary accruals *(DACC)* exercised by the sample companies were computed for period 2019–20 to 2023–24. The mean values of these indicators are presented in Table 4.3 and DACC values are displayed in Figure 4.3.

TABLE 4.3 TACC and DACC's means, for the sample companies, 2019–20 to 2023–24

Company	*TACCi* *Mean values*	*DACCi* *Mean values*
A	-4092.43	-0.01
B	379.11	0.01
C	-819.80	0.00
D	303.84	0.01
E	490.50	0.03
F	260.27	0.02
G	37.67	0.01
H	43.65	0.01
I	-922.48	-0.03
J	-205.81	0.02

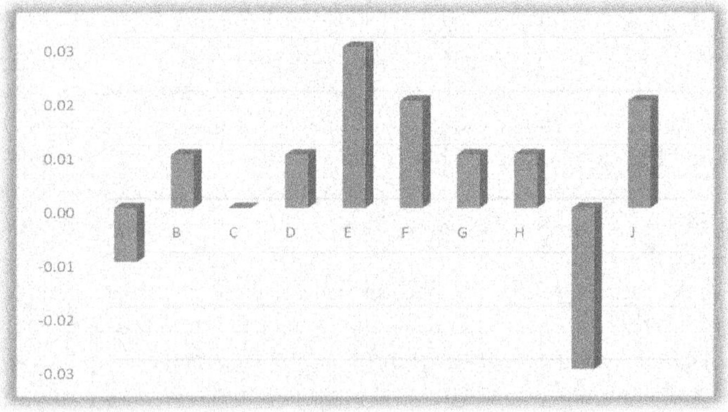

FIGURE 4.3 Discretionary accruals (DACC) for the sample companies, 2019–20 to 2023–24

An examination of Table 4.3 shows a definite presence of accrual management in all the sample companies, excluding "C." Company E has the highest average of discretionary accruals of 0.03 among all the units, whereas Company C has shown an almost zero average of discretionary accruals during the period. Most of the units have been found to be exercising income-increasing discretionary accruals, as verified by their positive average.

In Company A, the discretionary accruals average is negative at -0.01, indicating that managers are making income-decreasing accrual decisions. Total accruals trend has also been negative with an average of -4092.4, which indicates that apart from discretionary accruals, non-discretionary accruals exercised by the management have also been on the negative side. In Company B, the result is opposite to the former unit. Here, the trend in discretionary and total accruals both is found to be positive, as verified by their positive average of 0.01 and 379.11. It indicates managers are making income-increasing accrual decisions. Also, non-discretionary accruals are on a positive side. Company C comes out reasonably clean with almost zero average discretionary accruals during the period. The total accruals' average is negative at -819.80, indicating that non-discretionary accruals exercised have been on the negative side.

In the case of D, again the trend in discretionary and total accruals both is found to be positive, as verified by their positive average of 0.01 and 303.84. It indicates managers are making income-increasing accrual decisions. Also, non-discretionary accruals are on a positive side. Company E also indicates the income-increasing accruals with a discretionary accruals average of 0.03. It is equally true for non-discretionary accruals, and it can be verified by the total accruals average of 490.50. Company F takes the trend of income-increasing accruals further with a discretionary accruals average of 0.02. Also, non-discretionary accruals are on the positive side, as verified by total accruals' average of 260.27.

In Company G, the trend in discretionary accruals has been like the former unit. They have a positive discretionary accruals average of 0.01, indicating that managers are making income-increasing accrual decisions. Total accruals trend has also been positive with an average of 37.67, which indicates that apart from discretionary accruals, non-discretionary accruals exercised by the management have also been on the positive side. In Company H, the result is similar to the former unit. Here, the trend in discretionary and total accruals is again found to be positive, as verified by their positive averages of 0.01 and 43.65. It indicates managers are making income-increasing accrual decisions. In the case of Company I, the discretionary accruals' trend is negative, with an average of –0.03. It indicates managers are making income-decreasing accrual decisions. Non-discretionary accruals are also on the negative side, as verified by the total accruals' average of –922.48. The last Company J comes out with a positive average discretionary accruals of 0.02, indicating income-increasing accruals exercised by the management. But total accruals' average is negative at –205.81, indicating that non-discretionary accruals exercised have been on the negative side.

4.5 Industry smoothing (manipulation)

In the preceding discussion, we have examined the discretionary accruals trend in the sample units on an individual basis. In the subsequent discussion, we will attempt to explore this further on related aspects of industry income smoothing. The effects of the industry classification on income manipulation also need to be tested specifically. Accordingly, this study attempts to discover whether the behaviour of managers in service sectors differs from managers in non-service sectors regarding goal-directed determination of the cues and signals conveyed to users of financial statements through income numbers.

These motivational factors for financial shenanigans stem from management's desire to reduce environmental uncertainty and the significant swings in the company's operating performance, which are prone to sporadic cycles of good and bad times. There may be a number of organisational characteristics that set various firms apart along the smoothing attempt dimension. The "industry structure" is divided into two distinct categories, as the "manufacturing" and "service," according to economic dualism.

Economies tend to follow a developmental progression that takes them from a heavy reliance on agriculture, towards the development of manufacturing (e.g., textiles, automobiles, steel, aluminium) and finally towards a service-based structure. Thus, the non-service sector includes manufacturing and construction industries here. These firms are noted for high productivity, high profits, intensive utilisation of capital, high incidence of monopoly elements, and a high degree of unionisation. Generally, service sector firms face higher degrees of environmental uncertainty and a restricted opportunity structure and therefore are more predisposed to manage earnings than non-service sector firms. The environmental uncertainty is more evident with regard to the market for labour.

Firms in the service industry have more opportunities and more predisposition to smooth both their operating flows (e.g., through their labour management) and reported income measures than firms in the non-service sector. In other words, the two economic sectors rely on their differential ability to design profits.

This classification into a *service* and a *non-service (manufacturing)* group resulted in two firms in the service sector and eight firms in the non-service sector.

The income smoothing trend predicts a positive discretionary accrual performance in the service sector, on an average basis. Two service firms (D and E) are exercising income-increasing management. This leads to the fact that the service sector is inclined towards higher result-orientation for future uncertainties. Their nature of business operations is such that they tend to follow a "hike-and-spike" approach.

In the non-service sector, the units are mostly engaged in income-increasing management. But unlike the service sector, this group tends to be engaged in income-decreasing exercise as well. Company A and I have a negative discretionary performance of −0.01 and −0.03, respectively. It substantiates the relevance of timing and phase of the company deciding its accounting choices in the non-service sector.

An overall summary of the results shows the significant differences in the extent to which firms in the service sector and the non-service sector may be smoothing income due to differences in opportunity structures, experiences, and environmental uncertainty.

4.6 Beneish score of manipulation

The earnings manipulation detection in the units under study is presented below. The manipulation score was computed using the Beneish model for the period 2019–20 to 2023–24. The respective *P* scores are presented in Table 4.4 and Figure 4.4, and the weighted indices are presented in Appendix III.

P score allows a distinction between best performing firms and poorly performing firms and better and more efficient resource allocation for stakeholders. The choice-based exercise by the managers in financial reporting and their estimates to reflect the firm's true economic picture is well reflected.

An examination of Table 4.4 and Appendix III shows diverse variations in the p score of the sample companies. The evidence indicates that absolute *P* values of given companies are in a safer zone, being less than –1.78. But there is a probability of manipulation in individual weighted variables which increases with: (i) unusual increases in receivables, (ii) deteriorating gross margins, (iii) decreasing asset quality, (iv) sales growth, and (v) increasing accruals.

A Ltd. has shown a zero probability throughout the period, except for the current year 2023–24 at 0.01. Its DSRI has been almost linear during the first four years. But in the current year, 2023–24 it has increased tremendously to 1.16. A large increase in this index could be the result of a change in credit policy to spur sales in the face of increased competition, but such a disproportionate increase could also suggest revenue inflation. GMI shows a fluctuating trend. This is a negative signal about the company's prospects. Companies with poor prospects are

TABLE 4.4 Beneish profit model for the sample companies, 2019–20 to 2023–24 (P manipulation score)

Company	*2019–20*	*2020–21*	*2021–22*	*2022–23*	*2023–24*
1. A Ltd.	−2.80	−2.88	−3.22	−2.84	−2.37
2. B Ltd.	−2.04	−1.87	−3.36	−2.59	−1.91
3. C Ltd.	−3.16	−3.35	−2.77	−3.03	−3.44
4. D Ltd.	−2.51	−2.66	−3.10	−2.82	−2.89
5. E Ltd.	−2.54	−3.01	−2.66	−2.94	−2.76
6. F Ltd.	−2.67	−2.09	−3.12	−2.98	−2.93
7. G Ltd.	−3.01	−2.79	−2.72	−2.51	−2.61
8. H Ltd.	−3.17	−3.12	−2.64	−3.12	−2.69
9. I Ltd.	−3.33	−2.90	−3.31	−2.76	−2.31
10. J Ltd.	−3.01	−3.07	−2.93	−2.99	−2.93

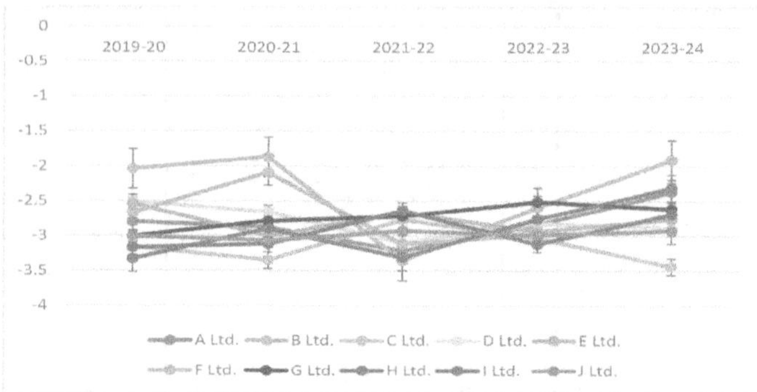

FIGURE 4.4 P score for the sample companies, 2019–20 to 2023–24

more likely to engage in earnings manipulation. AQI has shown a declining trend for the initial three years, but from the third year, it increased and has been constant for the last two years at 0.875. The ratio is still well under 1, which indicates not much of a cost deferral by the company. SGI has been more or less constant during the period around 1. TATA index has indicated a negative variable trend. It signifies a large change (decrease) in non-cash working capital of the firm. So, it is assumed that manipulation of financial information takes place in parts.

In the case of B Ltd., the average probability is 0.02. It has shown quite a fluctuating trend during the period. For 2019–20 and 2020–21, it has indicated chances of manipulation with an average score of 0.025. Its DSRI has followed quite a linear structure during the period. This index has decreased from 1.05 in 2019–20 to 0.69 in 2023–24. Such a significant decrease in this index is not desirable either and requires concern for managing revenues. GMI has also been very fluctuating here. In 2021–22, it is the worst at 0.35. Such a higher shrink in the ratio indicates that the risk is higher that management will engage in manipulation to create artificial profits or decrease losses. AQI has shown a declining trend for four years in a row, with the exception of the current year at 1.22. This is a little concern which indicates the company's propensity to capitalise costs. SGI has fluctuated during the period, showing an unstable level of sales which may or may not be real. TATA index has indicated a negative variable trend. So, it signifies a large change (decrease) in non-cash working capital of the firm. The chances of manipulation of financial information are evident.

Company C not only has an average probability of 0 but is able to maintain it throughout the time period under study. Its DSRI has followed an increasing trend until 2023–24. GMI has also more or less shown an increasing trend. AQI has shown a declining trend during the period. It declined from 1.01 in 2019–20 to 0.23 in 2023–24. SGI has been well around 1 during the period. TATA index has indicated a negative increasing value trend during 2022–23 to 2023–24. It indicated a large decrease in non-cash working capital of the firm. The chances of manipulation of financial information are negligible.

In D Ltd., the average probability is almost zero. Its DSRI has been more or less linear during the period. Its GMI has been quite stable around 0.90. AQI has shown a fluctuating trend. But the ratio is still below 1, which indicates chances of cost deferral by the company are low. SGI has not volatilised much during the period. TATA index has indicated a high negative variable trend. It signifies a large change (decrease) in non-cash working capital of the firm. But the effect of this variable has been set off by other variables, as evident in zero average probability.

E Ltd. has the same trend as Company D. Its average probability is zero. Its DSRI has been quite linear during the period. Its GMI has also shown a little fluctuating trend. AQI has shown a continuous decreasing trend. It decreased from 0.77 in 2019–20 to 0.43 in 2023–24. The positive part is that the ratio is well below 1, which indicates low chances of cost deferral by the company. SGI has been more or less constant during the period around 1. TATA index has indicated a negative variable trend. It signifies a change (decrease) in non-cash working capital of the firm. Here, traces of financial manipulation chances are almost negligible.

Company F has quite a low average probability of 0.02. Only for 2020–21, it was 0.02, and some chances of manipulation and its DSRI too have presented an unstable trend during the period. Revenue play cannot be ruled out. GMI has shown a stable trend and has stayed around 0.89. AQI has shown a declining trend. It declined from 0.92 in 2019–20 to 0.53 in 2023–24. The ratio is still well under 1 which indicates a low probability of capitalisation of costs. SGI has fluctuated but not much during the period, around 0.90. TATA index has indicated a negative variable trend. In the current year, i.e., 2023–24, it increased significantly to 0.05. So, it signifies a large change (decrease) in non-cash working capital of the firm. The chances of manipulation of financial information are evident.

In case of G Ltd., the average probability is 0. Its DSRI has followed an increasing trend for the first three years. It increased from 0.66 in 2019–20 to 1.09 in 2021–22, with an exception of a decline in 2022–23 at 0.62. The increase in this index is positive. GMI has fluctuated quite here. AQI has shown a moderate increasing trend. The ratio is still well under 1 which indicates not much cost capitalisation by the company. SGI has shown a high fluctuating trend during the period. Its index was highest at 1.14 in 2022–23. Such an increase in the index reflects a rise in sales which may or may not be real. TATA index has indicated a negative variable trend but only for three years. So, it signifies a decrease in non-cash working capital of the firm but not enormous. Manipulation of financial information is indicated but on a much lower side.

H Ltd. has a perfect picture with an average of 0, though its DSRI has been declining; GMI has also been very fluctuating here. In 2006–07, it is the worst at 0.35. AQI has shown a fluctuating trend over the past two years. The ratio is still well under 1, which indicates not much of the company's practice to capitalise costs. SGI has been more or less constant during the period around 1, except in 2023–24. Any further increase in the index reflects a rise in sales which may not be realistic. TATA index has indicated a negative variable trend. So, it signifies a change (decrease) in non-cash working capital of the firm. The chances of manipulation of financial information are indicated.

In case of I Ltd., the average probability is 0. Its DSRI has followed quite a non- linear structure during the period. This index was highest at 1.14 in 2023–24. Such a significant increase in this index indicates revenue manipulation. GMI has also been very fluctuating here. In 2019–20, it was the worst at 0.32. AQI has also shown a fluctuating trend. The overall ratio has been well under 1 which indicates less propensity to capitalise costs. SGI has shown almost a decreasing trend during the period, but it remained more or less around 1. TATA index has indicated a negative variable trend. So, it signifies a decrease in non-cash working capital of the firm. The chances of manipulation of financial information are evident.

In the case of J Ltd., the average probability is 0. Its DSRI has followed quite a non-linear structure during the period, though it stayed below 1. GMI has also been fluctuating here. AQI has shown a declining trend. It declined from 0.74 in 2019–20 to 0.61 in 2023–24. The ratio is still well under 1 which indicates the company's propensity to capitalise costs on the lower side. SGI has been more or less fluctuated during the period around 1. TATA index has indicated a negative variable trend for three years. It signifies a change (decrease), not much in non-cash working capital of the firm. Manipulation of financial information is just there.

5

DETECTION AND PREVENTION OF FINANCIAL FRAUDS

How to smell a rat?

Once the dataset has been examined using forensic tools and techniques that indicate a "red flag," you can send in the auditors and investigators and target the concerned stakeholders more effectively on questionable records. To probe and research the financial manipulation at hand in a better way, it is necessary to review the existing relevant financial statements and documents. The primary purpose of this review is to summarise the implications of forensic evidence on financial shenanigans to assess their pervasiveness and the overall integrity of financial reporting in corporate enterprises. Consequently, it's crucial to know which datasets are appropriate to compare to it and which are not as part of a detailed fraud detection process. This has important ramifications for different participants in the financial markets – investors, financial analysts, auditors, regulators, financial institutions, academia, and the business firms themselves. *The present chapter takes us to the next and final section of forensic accounting, whereby it reviews the significant grey areas of financial statements minutely – the indicators that are used for these financial shenanigans and how they affect shareholders' value?*

5.1 How to fix financial shenanigans: The forensic accounting way!

Forensic accounting framework for the detection and prevention of financial shenanigans is based on a creative accounting line

DOI: 10.4324/9781003730187-5

of items, as reflected in financial statements. The financial statements and various options available under GAAP for creative accounting are discussed below.

5.1.1 Income statement

A standard "statement of profit and loss" or "income statement" of a corporate enterprise is presented in Figure 5.1.

1 Income/Revenue

It consists generally of sales, fees, interest, dividends, and rents, while gains and losses comprise many types resulting from the

Statement of Profit and Loss of ABC Ltd. for the year ended 31st March, 2024

(INR in million)

Particulars	Note No.	2023–24	2022–23
REVENUE			
Revenue from operations			
Other income			
TOTAL INCOME			
EXPENSES			
Cost of material consumed			
Changes in inventories of finished goods, work in progress & scrap			
Employee benefits expense			
Finance costs			
Depreciation and amortisation expense			
Other expenses			
TOTAL EXPENSES			
Profit before tax			
Tax expense			
Profit for the year (Profit after tax - PAT)			

Significant accounting policies
Notes to the financial statements

FIGURE 5.1 Statement of profit and loss

sale of investments, sale of plant assets, settlement of liabilities, write-off of assets due to obsolescence or casualty, and theft.

The income figures are much affected by the type of accounting methods in general and allocation methods in particular. One can only imagine how shocked professionals, authors, and academics who signed "net profit contracts" for successful projects would be to learn later that the project was declared a loss due to the hiring agency's innovative overhead cost allocation.

2 Expenses

The expenses consist of the cost of goods sold, depreciation, interest, rent, salaries and wages, and taxes.

> Financial shenanigans or creative accounting blur the distinction between revenues and gains, and between expenses and losses to highlight a different performance between operating activities and non-operating activities. *For example,* loss-reporting dotcom firms may want to highlight a positive gross margin by shifting some product costs to period costs or to unusual activities.

3 Profit after tax (PAT)

The bottom figure of "net income" for the year often does not necessarily reveal the real picture. More useful insights are revealed from a segregation of results from regular continuing operations from the results of nonrecurring activities. These non-operating or non-recurring gains may not always be sustainable.

5.1.2 The balance sheet

A specimen balance sheet of a corporate enterprise is presented in Figure 5.2.

Balance Sheet of ABC Ltd. as at 31st March, 2024

(INR in million)

Particulars	Note No.	2024	2023
ASSETS			
(1) Non-Current Assets			
Property, plant and equipment			
Capital work-in-progress			
Investment property			
Intangible assets			
Intangible assets under development			
Financial assets*			
Deferred tax assets			
Other non-current assets			
(2) Current Assets			
Inventories			
Financial assets			
(i) Trade receivables			
(ii) Cash & Cash equivalents			
(iii) Bank balances			
(iv) Loans			
(v) Other financial assets			
Other current assets			
TOTAL			
EQUITY AND LIABILITIES			
EQUITY			
(1) Equity Share Capital			
(2) Other Equity (Reserves and Surplus)			
LIABILITIES			
(1) Non-Current Liabilities			
Financial liabilities**			
Provisions			
Other non-current liabilities			
(2) Current Liabilities			
Financial liabilities			
(i) Trade payables			
(ii) Other financial liabilities			
Other current liabilities			
Provisions			
TOTAL			

Significant accounting policies
Notes to the financial statements

FIGURE 5.2 Balance sheet

1 Basis

The balance sheet is supposed to be a reflection of the financial structure of the firm. Unfortunately, the majority of assets and liabilities are valued using "historical cost." The present values of the assets and liabilities, along with important non-quantitative data, are absent. The historical cost basis is essentially a "creative accounting" tool that is employed for practical and verifiable reasons in order to avoid displaying the firm's "fair value."

> The balance sheet is a stock concept, portraying the financial position at a point in time, which is the end of the fiscal year. Between the end of the year and issuance of the balance sheet, subsequent events or post-balance sheet events need to be disclosed in the notes. These events generally provide evidence about conditions that (i) either existed at the balance sheet, affect the estimates used in preparing financial statements, and call for additional adjustments or (ii) existed after the balance sheet date and call for additional disclosure.
>
> *Examples: (i) bonus issue; stock split or reverse split.*
>
> *(ii) loss of plant or inventories from fire or flood.*
>
> These get applied subjectively, as a part of creative accounting.

2 Assets

The assets are segregated into non-current (fixed) and current assets, where the rule of thumb is that if an asset is to be turned into cash or to be used to pay a current liability within a year of the operating cycle, whichever is longer, that asset is considered a current asset. The classification scheme is subject to discretion and can easily be used as a form of financial shenanigan.

3 Liabilities

Like assets, liabilities can be classified or measured according to different options and refinements available within generally accepted accounting principles and therefore are practically a tool for financial shenanigans.

5.2 Forensic accounting "red flags – digging"

The major items that are used for decoding financial shenanigans as forensic accounting "red flags" are explained as follows:

5.2.1 Revenue recognition

Revenue recognition means that the revenues have been both realised and earned. The timing of recognition is (i) the date of sale for the product sales from an inventory, (ii) services performed and billable for rendering a service, (iii) the passage of time or use of an asset, and (iv) date of sale for the sale of assets other than inventory.

However, departures from the sales basis are frequent and need to be justified.

1. For revenue recognised at a point of sale, creative accounting may be exercised in situations: (i) sales when the right of return exists, and (ii) trade in place and channel surfing.
2. For service or long-term construction contracts, revenue is recognised before delivery using either (i) the percentage-of-completion method or (ii) the completed-contract method.

When using the percentage-of-completion method, the determination of the progress towards completion is based on judgemental techniques such as the *cost-to-cost method, work performed method, etc.*

5.2.2 Depreciation

Depreciation is a way of allocating the cost of a tangible asset over the estimated life of the asset. It requires a judgement on (i) the appropriate, systematic, and rational way of allocation and (ii) an estimate of the useful life of the asset.

1. Though the estimation of the useful life is supposed to take into account physical factors (physical life) and economic factors (such as obsolescence), there may be arbitrary decisions in this exercise.
2. Depreciation methods include the (i) straight-line method, (ii) declining-balance method and decreasing change accelerated methods such as sum-of-the-year's digits, and (iii) special depreciation methods such as group and composite methods and hybrid combination methods.

The selection of a method is supposed to be based on securing the best matching of revenues and expenses. Other considerations such as practicality, lowering of taxes, and creative accounting may predominate.

5.2.3 Income taxes

Deferred tax assets and deferred tax liabilities are recognised as a result of the differences between pretax accounting income and taxable income. The amount of the deferred tax asset that will not be realised and must be recognised by a valuation allowance requires judgement.

5.2.4 Shareholders' funds

The costs of issuing stocks may be (i) debited to paid-in capital in excess of par or stated value, as a reduction of the amounts paid-in, or (ii) capitalised as an organisation cost and expensed over an arbitrarily decided time.

1. Stock issued for services or property other than cash is valued at the more clearly determinable fair value of the stock issued or fair market value of the non-cash consideration received.

   Selecting the fair market value of the non-cash consideration received could result in decisions that either overvalue the assets, creating "watered stock," or undervalue them, creating "secret reserves."

2. A separable disclosure is needed for redeemable preferred stock, non-redeemable preferred stock, and common stock.

5.2.5 Other equity/retained earnings

Whenever appropriation of retained earnings takes place, the firm should offer an adequate explanation for the action taken.

1. Restrictions on payment of dividends and other distributions to owners may exist for firms. Adequate disclosures about these restrictions and the legality of dividends are required.
2. Information on dividend policy warrants disclosure.

5.2.6 Property, plant, and equipment

Property, plant, and equipment or fixed assets are valued at historical cost, which fails to account for changes in specific and general price levels.

1. Judgement and creativity may be used for the capitalisation of costs subsequent to acquisition, such as additions, improvements and replacements, rearrangement and reinstallation, and repairs. *As an example,* if the repairs are ordinary, the change is expensed; however, if the judgement is that it is major, it is capitalised.

5.2.7 Intangible assets

Intangibles, such as patents, copyrights, trademarks, or goodwill, are characterised by both the lack of physical evidence and the degree of uncertainty concerning future benefits.

1. The product and process patents are amortised over the legal life or the useful life, whichever is shorter. Furthermore,

the patents include the capitalisation of legal fees. Legal fees and useful life calculations are left up to decisions that encourage innovative accounting solutions.
2. The legal life of copyrights is not a guarantee dial; the firm may choose a shorter period of time to amortise the copyrights.
3. The operating losses incurred in the early years by a developing-stage firm can be capitalised by some firms, although expensing makes more sense.
4. Goodwill is the difference between the purchase price and the fair market value of the assets. Both its valuation and the choice of the amortisation period create various scenarios for financial shenanigans.

5.2.8 Investments

Various classification schemes are needed to account for investments that tend to create opportunities for creative accounting.

1. Debt securities can be classified as (i) held-to-maturity, (ii) trading securities, or (iii) others. As such, the classification judgement has an impact on the level of income reported.
2. Equity securities are also classified as either available-for-sale or trading securities. The unrealised gains and losses are also recognised in net income for trading equity securities.

5.2.9 Inventory

For a manufacturing concern, inventories refer to finished goods, work-in-process, and raw materials. There may also be a separate inventory of manufacturing or factory supplies. It would be more instructive to properly segregate the firm's items rather than disclose a single inventory amount.

1. Product costs are "attached" to the inventory, while the selling and administrative expenses are charged as period costs. While it is easy to consider direct material and direct labour

as product costs, the manufacturing overhead costs are allocated. Some of these costs may be "improperly" treated as period costs in an effort to "boost" the level of gross margin.

2. Cost-flow assumptions include (i) the specific identification method, (ii) the average cost method, and (iii) the first-in, first-out method (FIFO). The cost-flow assumptions may not necessarily be consistent with the flow of goods, and other considerations may prevail.
3. Inventories are valued on the basis of the lower of cost or market. It is always considerate to make discretionary estimates.

5.2.10 Receivables

There are trade receivables and non-trade receivables. The trade receivables are accounts receivable from customers who arise in the normal course of business.

Non-trade receivables include (i) advances to employees and subsidiaries, (ii) deposits as guarantees of performance in payments, and (iii) claims.

1. Receivables are valued and reported at the net realisable value, which is what is expected to be received in cash. This requires the estimation of both uncollectible receivables and any returns and allowances to be granted.
2. Creative accounting is possible in the classification of receivables if there are "failures" in the segregation of different types of receivables, or the disclosure of any loss contingencies on receivables, or the disclosure of receivables pledged as collateral.

5.2.11 Cash

Cash consists of currency, available funds on deposits at the bank, and negotiable instruments such as certified cheques, bank drafts, and money market funds.

1. Every firm is to maintain a minimum cash balance in checking or savings accounts. These legally restructured deposits need to be disclosed separately among the "cash and cash equivalent items" in current assets.

Any misclassification of accounts cited above is merely an attempt at Financial shenanigan.

5.2.12 Non-current/long-term debt

Long-term debt is issued with specific covenants and restrictions stated in the bond indenture or note agreement. Their disclosure in the notes is crucial. Failure to do so defeats the full disclosure principle.

1. Due to differences between the stated rate or coupon rate and the market or effective rate, bonds are issued at either a premium or a discount. The amortisation of the discount or premium may be based on either the effective interest method or the straight-line method.
2. The debt issue costs are generally capitalised, then amortised.
3. Firms may try to acquire debt and avoid recording the obligations on the balance sheet through various forms of off-balance-sheet financing. This may be easily accomplished by two entities, A and B, forming a new entity CD that borrows funds that are guaranteed by the firms A and B. In this case, A and B have incurred more debt but do not appear on their balance sheets. The agreement with the new entity may include either a take-or-pay contract or a throughput agreement. These off-balance-sheet financing schemes are prominent examples of financial shenanigan schemes.

5.2.13 Current liabilities

Current liabilities are obligations whose liquidation is expected to have a maturity within one year of the operating cycle. The account will not be comparable from one industry to another given the different operating cycles adopted.

1. Both the maturing portion of long-term debt and a liability that is due within a year (or operating cycle) should be classified as a current liability. Any other long-term debt classified as current liabilities is a form of financial shenanigan.
2. Litigations, claims, and assessments, as well as unfiled suits and unasserted claims whose outcomes can be predicted, need to be recognised by a liability. Failure to do so is clearly a manifestation of a discretionary element.

So, there are various possibilities of financial shenanigans as identified above in the form of key "red flags" in financial statements. The creativity is generally a by-product of the flexibility and the variety of options available within GAAP as well as the result of a very "liberal" interpretation of the accounting rules.

QUICK CHECK!

The potential red dots, usually invisible in the financial statements, that emerge from the preceding discussion can be grouped as:

- Unusual rise in accounts receivable relative to sales growth (expanding sales channels or easing credit to increase profits).
- Unexplained accounting adjustments, particularly when performance is poor (e.g., change from accelerated to straight-line depreciation).
- Unknown transactions that increase profit (e.g., sale of assets).
- Increasing gap between Net Income and Cash Flow from Operations (firm might be "fiddling around" with accruals).

6
CORPORATE FIASCOS

"Charles Ponzi," who relished his life to the fullest until his incarceration, deserves the ultimate credit for the conception of these scams. He was a con man and businessman from Italy. Ponzi achieved popularity in America with his notorious "Ponzi Scheme," in which he defrauded thousands of investors out of roughly $32 million in the early 1920s – an amount that would today be worth nearly half a trillion dollars. *The case evidence(s) of the financial manipulation framework in this chapter is based on 15 major corporate frauds that have occurred over the years. Based on the "driving action" by the management from the front seat of frauds, where others may have undoubtedly assisted it, it detects the "rotting" cycle in the situations.*

6.1 WorldCom (2002)

In the USA, WorldCom was a telecom provider. The telecom behemoth that is now known as MCI committed a staggering $11 billion in asset inflation, which resulted in $180 billion in losses for investors and the loss of 30,000 jobs.

It was discovered that the chief offender, CEO Bernie Ebbers, had inflated revenues through false accounting entries and underreported line costs by capitalising expenditures rather than reducing them. He was given a 25-year sentence for conspiracy, fraud, and the submission of false paperwork. The controller resigned, the CFO lost his job, and the company declared

DOI: 10.4324/9781003730187-6

bankruptcy. January 2006 saw Verizon Communications purchase it; it is currently MCI!

"It comes down to leadership." The board of directors should be the ones to support people without closely examining them and making sure they are qualified before they join the C-suite. Bernie played the catalyst behind the scam. His past performance indicates that he was not a good match for the role. His experience wasn't enough for a CEO. In essence, his business strategy counted on continuous expansion leading to rising stock prices. That has a lot of problems, and a responsible CEO would never allow that.

6.2 Managing Waste (2002)

This publicly traded company, which has its headquarters in Houston, is charged with falsifying its earnings statements by $1.7 billion and extending the time that its property, plant, and equipment take to depreciate on the balance sheets. The Securities Exchange Commission (SEC) brought accusations against it in 2002, and a shareholder class-action lawsuit resulting in a $457 million fine resolved the matter.

The mastermind behind this scam from the front, President Philip Rooney, ensured that required write-offs were not recorded and, in certain situations, turned down accounting decisions that would have a detrimental impact on company operations. He obtained about $9.2 million in fraudulent proceeds from the sale of company stock, retirement benefits, and performance-based bonuses during the crime.

The plan's execution was mostly the responsibility of CFO James Koenig. He gained nearly $900,000 by engaging in dishonest behaviour. Thomas Hau, the CEO and corporate controller, methodically created the false disclosures and devised many "one-off" accounting techniques to generate the targeted profits. He profited by more than $600,000.

As a result, the defendants were charged with concealing their scheme through various means, such as making false and misleading statements about the company's accounting practices, financial status, and future prospects in press releases, shareholder reports, and SEC filings. They were also accused of using accounting gimmicks to conceal their true performance from public view.

6.3 Enron (2002)

It was discovered that the American energy corporation Enron used "mark-to-market accounting." The Houston-based provider of commodities, energy, and services was able to keep sizable loans off its balance sheets. The corporation filed for Chapter 11 bankruptcy, resulting in the loss of $74 billion for stockholders as well as thousands of employees' retirement plans and jobs.

The company's primary financial ploys include fabricating fake special purpose companies (SPEs), generating virtual profits, and gaining the confidence of the markets by making large payments to banks and analysts prior to the fraud's exposure in 2001. Enron declared $20 billion in total revenues in 1997; by 2000, those revenues had increased to $101 billion, a fivefold increase! Enron was the second-biggest client for auditor Arthur Andersen, with an annual charge exceeding $52 million. It had a significant role in the business as a consultant and auditor.

When rising stock prices fuelled rumours of misconduct, senior executive Sherron Watkins sounded the alarm. The CEO, Jeff Skilling, was sentenced to 24 years in prison. The chairman, Kenneth Lay, passed away prior to receiving a punishment. After entering a guilty plea to two conspiracy counts, serving time in prison, and forfeiting $24 million, the former CFO Andrew Fastow stated, "There are people who look at the rules and find ways to structure around them." Fastow was the one operating the fraudulent ship and making at least $30 million in "fees" through SPEs.

6.4 Tyco (2002)

This New Jersey-based Swiss security systems company was accused in 2002 of using questionable accounting practices to inflate the company's income by $500 million and give the CEO and CFO personal wealth of $150 million. The money was stolen through fake stock transactions and illegal loans, all done under the guise of executive incentives and benefits.

$74 billion was lost by stockholders. "An externally managed anonymous top line is the best option for a typical organisation, but it typically fails due to a conflict of interest that makes it impossible for it to be handled internally and addressed."

CEO L. Dennis Kozlowski and CFO Mark Swartz were sentenced to 8 to 25 years in prison. As a result of a class-action lawsuit, the company was ordered to repay investors $2.92 billion. During the peak of the controversy, Kozlowski spent $2 million hosting a party for his wife on a private island, which featured a performance by Jimmy Buffett. The company published a report detailing how he used corporate cash to remodel and refurbish his Fifth Avenue apartment in New York, which cost $14 million.

6.5 Adelphia Communications (2002)

The listed business was headed by a family, and the family embezzled funds from the business. On 27 March 2002, Adelphia authorities announced that co-borrowings under the family's private trust, Highland Holdings, between Adelphia and other Rigas family firms had accrued $2.3 billion in unrecorded debt; accusations were made against Adelphia Communications Corp., its founder John J. Rigas, his three sons, and two senior executives.

In order to satisfy Wall Street's expectations, Adelphia (i) falsely concealed liabilities worth billions of dollars on the books of off-balance sheet affiliates, (ii) overstated earnings, and (iii) concealed the Rigas Family's widespread self-dealing, which included the covert use of corporate funds for the purchase of opulent condominiums in New York and other locations.[1]

The aforementioned case paints a very unsettling image of greed and dishonesty within a sizable, publicly traded corporation. It was discovered that John and the other defendants persisted in their fraud even after Adelphia admitted it on 27 March 2002. In 2004, Adelphia made a reorganisation filing.

6.6 Freddie Mac (2003)

According to a 2003 SEC report, this enormous mortgage firm with federal support inflated its earnings by $5 billion. The business paid $125 million in fines and fired its CFO, COO, and CEO.

Vaughn A. Clarke, chief financial officer; David W. Glenn, president, chief operating officer, and vice chairman of the board; and former senior vice presidents are the charged former Freddie Mac executives. "As has been seen in so many cases, Freddie Mac's departure from proper accounting practices was the result of a corporate culture that sought stable earnings growth at any cost."[2]

The Freddie Mac board modified the company's bylaws, meeting schedule, and code of conduct. Information about Freddie Mac's internal controls and plans to strengthen its internal audit division, such as separating the chairman's and CEO's duties, was required. These weren't in place.

6.7 Parmalat (2003)

The Parmalat scam began as an attempt to hide losses, much like many other scams do. When the company's South American business began to lose money in 1990, CEO Calisto Tanzi made the decision to fabricate financial records in order to conceal the division's losses from the public. As is the case with many scams, Parmalat's decision to commit fraud made the company route dependent, which in turn fostered ever-more dishonest accounting practices and self-dealing. The fraud was eventually discovered after Parmalat's 2003 €150 million bond sale failed, despite the company having over €4 billion in cash and equivalents on its balance sheet.

Parmalat was founded in 1961 on a farm in Northern Italy that was run by a family. In the years that followed, the company grew steadily into a multinational conglomerate and rose to prominence as one of Italy's largest dairy and food companies. During its 2003 crisis, Parmalat identified 214 companies across 48 countries.

Over the course of these 13 years, from 1990 to 2003, they raised their profits by inventing fake transactions through the use of a double-billing approach. They took out more bank loans with the receivables from these fake sales serving as collateral. They created fake assets, inflating claimed assets. Examples of these financial engineering techniques are the following: *displaying net debt as $2.29 billion when the true amount is $18.0 billion, and reporting revenue as $6.77 billion when the actual revenue is $5.04.*

Parmalat was formally declared bankrupt on 27 December 2003, and CEO Calisto Tanzi was taken into custody on suspicion of fraud. Parmalat was relisted on the Milan exchange in 2005.

6.8 American Insurance Group (AIG) (2005)

The top global provider of business and individual insurance solutions was charged with $3.9 billion worth of accounting fraud, stock price manipulation, and bid-rigging.

AIG restated their earnings for the four years prior in May 2005, which resulted in a nearly $4 billion decrease in profits. The CEO, Hank Greenberg, told dealers to falsify stock values, reported loans as profits, and sent clients to insurers with which AIG had payback obligations. AIG was able to pay off to foreign banks the $62.1 billion that it might have owed to counterparties, thanks in large measure to Scott Alvarez. In terms of bid rigging, it was "one of the more sophisticated but also prevalent frauds."

For years, there were these warning signs. If an auditor used due diligence, they might easily spot this deception. Auditors don't seem to have learnt this lesson, though.

6.9 Lehman Brothers (2008)

A significant amount of this financial services company's debt liability was concealed as an off-balance-sheet item. Its unethical behaviour – passing off debts worth over $50 billion as sales – caused it to file for bankruptcy.

It was a team effort with many intricate causes rather than a one-man performance. In a nutshell, Lehman was too liquid and had too little collateral to borrow enough money from the Federal Reserve or to extend the repurchase agreement contracts (repos) in order to prevent a collapse. In essence, it was taking out a short-term borrowing from the future to correct the situation the following quarter, and so forth.

Lehman was a prime example of "I need to report an extra $20 million." It was a temporary theft from the future, intended to be made up in the following quarter, but it went on. Stronger rules for revenue recognition would be necessary, according to this.

6.10 Madoff (2008)

Madoff's Wall Street investment securities company conned investors out of $64.8 billion in the largest Ponzi scam in history. They were paid with money from other investors or their own, instead of giving investors returns on their gains.

The day after he faced redemptions of $7 billion and confessed his guilt to his sons, Madoff was turned over to the SEC. As the saying goes, "something is wrong when things are going too well."

Rich investors who could take the loss were not the only ones victimised by this; regular people were also duped out of their life savings.

6.11 Satyam (2009)

Satyam was a global software firm based in India that was discovered to have falsified employee and customer identities in order to inflate its balance sheet and overestimate profits and cash balances. A total of INR 50,400 million in false cash and bank balances, INR 3,760 million in non-existent accrued interest, INR 12,300 million in understated liabilities, and INR 21,610 million in exaggerated receivables contributed to the $1.5 billion inflation in earnings.

The founder and chairman of the company, Ramalinga Raju, acknowledged the deception in a letter to the board of directors. He and his brother were charged with conspiracy, cheating, record-faking, and breach of trust. Then he said that it had gotten out of control and compared the scenario to "riding a tiger, not knowing how to get off without being eaten." In 2009, Satyam was ultimately purchased by the Mahindra Group.

6.12 Kingfisher (2012)

One of the biggest scandals that damaged India's economy was Kingfisher Airlines, a costly INR 90,000 million affair perpetrated by Vijay Mallya. Even with all of his accomplishments, Vijay Mallya is most remembered for the scandal that followed the downfall of Kingfisher. Soon after its founding in 2005, Kingfisher became well-known. All of it was brought about by recently remodelled aircraft, friendly airline staff, delicious cuisine, and – most importantly – enjoyment of the in-flight experience in 2006.

Vijay Mallya continued to operate his aircraft firm by taking out bank loans. Vijay Mallya received loans totalling INR 90,000 million from 17 banks, and other banks kept giving him credit even after SBI declared him bankrupt. Money laundering and fraud charges were brought against Vijay Mallya. His business also collected traveller transport tax, PF, and employee income tax. He did not share these numbers with the IT or PF staff. The company was forced into bankruptcy as a result of its inability to pay staff wages.

Due to financial difficulties, Kingfisher was forced to close its doors in 2012, and in December of the same year, its permit was cancelled. Moreover, Vijay Mallya stopped repaying his obligation. The Kingfisher corporation was nearing the end of its existence at this point. The primary cause of the airline catastrophe was ineffective governance. At Kingfisher, there was never a permanent CEO or MD.

6.13 Toshiba (2015)

The Toshiba Corporation was a well-known Japanese company that produced electronics and computers for both consumers and business use. It ceased to exist as a publicly traded corporation on 20 December 2023, as a group led by Japan Industrial Partners (JIP) took it private.

Toshiba's issues began in 2015 when it revealed accounting irregularities involving several businesses and senior management. Over a seven-year period, it exaggerated pretax earnings by 230 billion yen ($1.59 billion). Following the discovery of more accounting errors at a fully owned subsidiary in January 2020, five activist shareholders' nominees for directors were rejected at an annual general meeting in July 2020.

The shareholders ousted board chairman Osamu Nagayama on 25 June 2021, citing the board's alleged failure to respond to allegations that it had exerted pressure on investors. Toshiba pledges to communicate with potential investors and carry out a comprehensive asset evaluation. Toshiba declared in November 2021 that it would split into three companies: an energy company, an infrastructure firm, and a management company for its stake in Kioxia. On 1 March 2022, CEO Satoshi Tsunakawa stepped down.

6.14 IL&FS (2018)

One of India's largest financial scandals was revealed to be Infrastructure Leasing & Finance Services Limited (IL&FS), with an estimated value of INR 990,000 million. It swung the balance of power away from the country's corporate regulators and accounting advocates. As soon as the scam was exposed, all of the authorities moved quickly to take corrective measures.

The country's accounting professional association, the Institute of Chartered Accountants of India (ICAI), announced the establishment of a committee to look into IL&FS issues and make suggestions. Subsequently, the ICAI released an updated set of codes of ethics in February 2019. The "National Guidelines on Responsible Business Conduct," published in March 2019 by the Ministry of Corporate Affairs of the Government of India, mandate that businesses conduct themselves in an "Ethical, Transparent, and Accountable" manner.

IL&FS Ltd. is the main investment firm and serves as the holding company for the IL&FS Group. The organisation worked in more than a dozen sectors within the service industry, including tourism, education, urban infrastructure, and transportation. The company appeared to be well-managed, with a knowledgeable board of directors.

The IL&FS management started taking out loans from all kinds of sources, secured and unsecured, which started the whole catastrophe. The exorbitant and illogical loans acquired from various financiers and investors ultimately turned into an indelible burden. They started to default on all debts, loans, and investor deposits all of a sudden. The very next day, after the rating agencies' deception was exposed, the company's credit ratings dropped. The issue was brought to light in July 2018 after two IL&FS entities, ITNL and IFIN, failed to repay loans and inter-corporate deposits to particular banks and lenders. Over the next few months, an increasing number of IL&FS Group companies filed for bankruptcy. Disregard for organisations and regulations took on a new chapter after the IL&FS group's abrupt default and public exposure.

As a result, IL&FS's reputation was ruined. Financial misappropriation and unlawful income diversion were held against the directors. Within a day of entering power, the government sacked the senior management of IL&FS and placed them in jail. Along with representatives from the government, a new board was constituted, consisting of prominent personalities from Indian finance and business.

6.15 Silicon Valley Bank (2023)

Silicon Valley Bank (SVB)'s sudden and widely reported failure on 10 March 2023, which involved hiding massive losses from regulators, investors, and depositors, is a sobering reminder of the threats corporate fraud poses to the US financial system.

These findings clearly show that, in order to prevent corporate fraud, better risk management and oversight are needed. A proposed class action was filed in federal court in San Jose, California, against SVB, Chief Financial Officer Daniel Beck, and Chief Executive Greg Becker.

SVB was said to have $175.4 billion in deposits and $209 billion in assets before it failed. Since the 2008 financial crisis, this was the largest bank collapse in the United States. Its failure has sparked fears of a contagion among other lenders serving wealthy clients, including big regional banks and venture-backed technological start-ups.

The fact that Silicon Valley Bank concentrated on lending money to startups in the biopharma and IT industries was what set it apart. It required deposits, just like other banks; however, in contrast to other banks, a sizable amount of these deposits came from software businesses with substantial funding. In order to offer its depositors a reasonable return on their money, the bank decided to place their funds in secure, long-term Treasury bonds. Everything was well until the Federal Reserve started raising interest rates significantly. Unfortunately, the bank was compelled to issue long-term, low-interest Treasury bonds in response to pressure to provide its depositors higher rates of return as a result of the interest rate hike. When depositors started pulling out of the bank in search of higher interest rates, the bank was forced to sell off some of its Treasury bonds at a loss. An increase in interest rates lowers the value of bonds.

A liquidity crisis, which arises when depositors withdraw money from banks more quickly than the banks can handle it, quickly befell the bank. The FDIC took over the bank after a "run on the bank" and said that all depositors would get their money back. First Citizens Bank purchased Silicon Valley Bank on 27 March 2023.

TABLE 6.1 Corporate fiasco portfolio

Company	*Year*	*Result*	*Country*
WorldCom	2002	Operational	US
Waste Management	2002	Operational	US
Enron	2002	Closed-down	US
Tyco	2002	Operational	US
Adelphia	2002	Operational	US
Freddie Mac	2003	Operational	US
Parmalat	2003	Operational	Italy
AIG	2005	Operational	US
Lehman Brothers	2008	Closed-down	US
Madoff Securities	2008	Closed-down	US
Satyam	2009	Operational	India
Kingfisher	2012	Closed-down	India
Toshiba	2015	Closed-down	Japan
IL&FS	2018	Operational	India
Silicon Valley Bank	2023	Operational	US

The above descriptive fiascos list is given in Table 6.1.

Thus, it is evident that while Enron and WorldCom are prime examples of financial shenanigans from the US, no country or economic system has a monopoly on accounting scandals, as the Parmalat (Italy), Toshiba (Japan), and Satyam and IL&FS (India) affairs prove.

References

1. https://www.sec.gov/news/press/2002-110.htm.
2. https://www.sec.gov/news/press/2007/2007-205.htm.

7

CASELETS

The present section discusses various caselets and examples of financial shenanigans for advanced learning.

7.1 A&B Inc. (an MNC) in computer hardware with "sales designing"

The listed Indian subsidiary reported a 65% CAGR in sales growth from FY21 to FY25. The company's management claims that it has been emphasising digitisation of documents and establishing paperless, effective procedures for other businesses. This resulted in driving supernormal sales growth.

But as sales increased, the company's working capital also skyrocketed. With additional sales, its working capital days rose to 180 days. Despite having a negative cash flow of INR 400 million, the company reported a cumulative EBITDA of INR 250 million.

> *This is a classic example of false revenue reporting. Companies must record revenues when earned and not just when money is received or contract signed. If a company reports very high growth in revenues but it is not backed by cashflows and the receivables are going up proportionately, investor should look into with more diligence.*

DOI: 10.4324/9781003730187-7

7.2 Z Ltd. in "accelerated sales"

In 2022, Z Ltd. was found to be involved in revenue recognition of equipment sales that resulted in a $2.5 billion increase in pre-tax earnings. The company moved those service revenues to the time of purchase, even though it was intended to record revenues both up front and over time (for servicing equipment over its usable life).

> *As a part of accounting principles, revenue should be recognized when the company delivers or performs the task to be paid for – not necessarily when the payment is received. This is revenue recognition principle.*

7.3 S Lon's "dramatic revenue and net profit"

In just three short years, S Lon's revenue had increased by an exponential factor of 5, growing from $1 billion in 2022 to $5.5 billion in 2025. As shown in Table 7.1, the company's dramatic revenue growth resulted in a big rise in net income as well, rather than an increase in revenue.

> *Rational investors would wonder how S Lon has increased its revenue from $1 million to more than $5 million in a three-year period. Without making any significant acquisitions along the way, the company could not achieve its extraordinary revenue growth. The unusual way the firm treated trading activities as sales was the root cause of the reported revenue growth. Additionally, by managing expenses more*

TABLE 7.1 S Lon's revenue and net income, 2020 to 2025

($ millions)	*2022*	*2023*	*2024*	*2025*
Revenue	1	2.2	3.8	5.5
Net Income	0.2	0.8	1.2	2.5

or less in the same percentage, they were also able to inflate the profits much higher than revenue.

7.4 Dreamz Media records "premature revenue"

In a subscription business, the subscription fees are paid to the business before the customer makes use of the services, whether they are TV subscriptions, prepaid mobile phones, or others. Dreamz Media records this as revenue when a customer pays a subscription fee of INR 15,000 annually. Revenues of INR 1,250 per month, pro rata, must be reported by the company as an ideal practice.

However, some businesses inflate their profits and record the entire amount on the receipt. This is booking revenues too soon to manipulate earnings.

7.5 A&B's – telecom companies' – "misaligned ARPU"

The ARPU (average revenue per user) by the management of company A excludes advertisement revenue and reports only subscription revenue, whereas the management of company B includes advertisement and other items as well. In this case, company B is able to fix up the sales liberally. Similarly, different companies may use different criteria to select the number of users for calculating ARPU.

The key here is what constitutes the revenue and the actual number of users in ARPU. It is often manipulated to hike sales by companies.

7.6 Bright Enterprises with "round-tripping"

Bright was engaging in round-trip trades with special purpose entities. It indulged in "overstatement of its gas-trading activity resulting from 'round-trip' or 'wash' trades – simultaneous, pre-arranged buy-sell trades of gas with the same counter-party, at the same price and volume, and over the same term, resulting in neither profit nor loss to either transacting party."

This is practice where a firm trades an asset and then buys it back multiple times to inflate its transaction volume and boosting the top line.

7.7 D Foods Ltd. involved in an "expense manipulation"

The company allegedly deferred the payments to Walls Inc. to later periods in order to offset costs during its fiscal 2023 year. This enabled them to inflate earnings as they entered into negotiations with a leading consumer goods company. The price of D Food's shares was crucial to the stock deal, which saw a big rise after the results.

Under accounting principles, expenses should be recognised when incurred – not necessarily when the payment is made as part of the recognition principle.

7.8 Fast-jumpers Ltd. "defer expenses"

Fast jumpers, being a new company with five years of operations, entail lowering costs and increasing profits for the current period by postponing booking expenses to the following period. They would not record the receipt of the invoice and kept it in an inbox until the beginning of the next period in order to delay the expenses.

Accounts payable is the most frequently underreported liability by them in an effort to strengthen a company's balance sheet. The way followed by them to remove accounts payable from the balance sheet was to wait until the audit was finished and conceal invoices for goods and services that were received from the auditor before year end.

To identify the signs, an eye should be kept for differences between the quantity of goods billed and the quantity shipped.

7.9 H Com's indulgence in "capitalisation of expenses"

H Com started capitalising billions in line costs as a telecommunications (telecom) company. A close examination of the Statement of Cash Flows would have revealed deteriorating free cash flow. Table 7.2 illustrates the remarkable $7.5 billion decline in free cash flow from a positive $2 billion in 2024 (the year prior to capitalising the line costs) to a negative $5.5 billion in 2025.

> *In particular, there are concerns about H Com's significant increase in capital expenditures as the telecom sector was collapsing and went against industry's guidance for relatively rising capital expenditures. Such rise in capital expenditures was, in fact, a manipulation; in fact, it was mostly the effort of company's altering its accounting policies to shift regular operating expenses, or line costs, to the balance sheet in order to inflate profits.*

7.10 Lit & Co. has "fast build of inventory"

Lit accumulates inventory, though it is outdated and no longer useful. The reason is that it would have to record impairment losses, which would lower earnings; management might be hesitant to write off such inventory.

Such significant avoidance has a significant impact on earnings, and it is undeniable that it helps the share price to maintain and not fall. However, if such write-offs are truly necessary, they cannot be postponed indefinitely, and businesses eventually realise significant impairment losses.

TABLE 7.2 H Com's free cash flow

($ millions)	*2024*	*2025*
Cash flow from operations (CFO)	10,000	6,000
Less: Capital expenditure	(8,000)	(11,500)
Free cash flow	2,000	(5,500)

So, when an investor encounters businesses with steadily declining inventory turnover over time, she should conduct additional due diligence to detect financial gimmick that businesses employ.

7.11 IOT Ltd.'s appearance of "assets pump-up"

IOT presents another well-known instance of income smoothing. In order to preserve the appearance of consistent growth, it inflated revenues by inflating its assets through revaluing their costs at regular intervals and misusing the "fair value" concept by hiking the present value of fixed assets, particularly tangible assets. As an outcome, at the time of overvalued assets, they could also charge high depreciation, leading to secret reserves. The net result was an increase in the net worth of the company and a good picture with the lenders and other stakeholders.

This instance highlights the dangers of in-house income smoothing since it can conceal underlying financial issues and have dire repercussions.

7.12 X Ltd. acquires Y Ltd. and shows "growth sign via CFO"

A common way for overly astute managers to cover up a lot of things is through acquisitions. Acquisitions give acquiring companies a lot of ways (loopholes) to make their books look nicer. CFO (cash flow from operating activities) improvement is one such weakness.

When received, the Y (the acquired company's) accounts receivable go through the acquirer's (X) CFO. However, the expenses incurred to create these receivables (the acquired company's purchased inventory, previous salaries, etc.) that should ideally go through the CFO as an outflow now pass through the CFI (cash flow from investing activities) as the acquiring company's acquisition cost. This happens because any company that attempts to grow organically would have to make significant

TABLE 7.3 Samy's first year depreciation

Purchase Year/ Series	*Purchase Price ($ millions)*	*Useful Life (years)*	*First Year Depreciation ($ millions)*
2010/MD-200	10	10	1
2011/MD-200	12	15	0.8
2012/MD-200	15	20	0.75
2013/MD-200	18	25	0.72

cash outflows from operations (inventory purchase, salaries, etc.) in order to generate cash inflow from operations (CFO). In contrast, in an acquisition, the acquiring company receives the target's future cash inflow from operations (outstanding account receivables at the time of acquisition), but the associated cash outflow (acquisition cost) is recorded as a cash outflow.

Therefore, acquisitions provide a common method of boosting CFO and showing growth.

7.13 Samy's "depreciation policy turnout"

Samy Corporation is involved in the manufacturing of heavy engines for commercial vehicles. The physical or economic life, planned uses, and anticipated technological changes are just a few of the many variables that are taken into account when estimating the economic life of its machinery for calculating depreciation using the straight-line method (SLM). Since 2010, Samy has extended the anticipated life of its aircraft by five years on four separate occasions. Extended lives may have made sense in the industry, but this led to lower annual depreciation amounts in order to report higher net income or reduce losses, as evident in Table 7.3.

Samy Lines has changed assumptions of economic life of the aircraft 4 times on similar series of machines, resulting in lower depreciation. This is not as per ethical standards.

7.14 Gen and Nit's "diverse opex treatment"

Gen and Nits are in the software development sector. Company Gen adheres to International Financial Reporting Standards (IFRS) by expensing $10,000 for research and capitalising $5,000 for development as an operating expense (opex). In contrast, Company Nits capitalises all $15,000 in identical expenses – avoiding the immediate recognition of research costs.

> *The above accounting choice allows Company Nit to report $10,000 less in operating expenses – making it appear more profitable than Company Gen despite not performing better.*

7.15 Edu Ltd. plays down "non-recurring expenses"

Non-recurring expenses play a crucial role in financial reporting as these one-time fees are meant to cover exceptional circumstances so that interested parties can make well-informed decisions. Edu Ltd. takes advantage of this accounting technique by consistently adding non-recurring costs of advisory fees to their annual financial reports. In the year 2025, after seven years, they discover that they have overestimated their reserves after a few quarters. Thus, they reverse some of the amount back into their income in the year's financial statements.

> *Businesses may give a false impression of their financial performance by carefully managing the inclusion and reversal of non-recurring expenses. Investors must critically evaluate the type and frequency of such expenses in a company's reporting in order to have a clear reflection of the financial picture of the company.*

7.16 High-ups show "off-balance sheet items"

Companies can create distinct subsidiaries to hide liabilities or expenses that the parent company wants to keep hidden in the complex world of financial reporting. High-ups during their last

10 years of operations have created 246 subsidiaries without having to be included in the parent company's financial statements, as they all were set up as separate legal entities. They were found to be concealing off-balance-sheet items, like guarantees from investors, by the regulators in 2024. They would also transfer assets and debt to these entities, giving the appearance of improved financial health and increased profitability.

Investors must be on the lookout for any off-balance-sheet entities and comprehend how they might affect the company's overall transparency and financial health.

7.17 Young Brothers Ltd.'s "disjoint analysis"

Young Brothers' financial performance has been deteriorating over time. Anomalies and patterns can be found by comparing its financial "profitability" ratios over time, exposing departures from historical norms that are not adequately explained.

Furthermore, as compared to its competitors, outliers in profit indicators are found with a huge margin on the negative side. These outliers act as warning signs that demand more investigation, whether they are going down gradually or declaring losses as part of a strategic approach.

Such disparities may indicate dishonest tactics intended to conceal the company's actual financial situation, requiring further investigation to identify the root causes.

APPENDIX

Appendix I

Quality of earnings for the sample companies, 2019–20 to 2023–24 *(Amount in INR crore, 1 crore = 100 million)*

(i) A Ltd					
	2019–20	**2020–21**	**2021–22**	**2022–23**	**2023–24**
Operating cash flow	11777.6	17288.58	10301.6	16870.6	17426.7
Net income	5160.14	7571.68	9069.34	11943.4	19458.3
Quality of earnings (%)	**228.24**	**228.33**	**113.59**	**141.25**	**89.56**
(ii) B Ltd					
	2019–20	**2020–21**	**2021–22**	**2022–23**	**2023–24**
Operating cash flow	240.9	−347.93	725.8	−819.38	855.42
Net income	197.15	106.42	511.12	784.03	951.63
Quality of earnings (%)	**122.19**	**−326.94**	**142.00**	**−104.51**	**89.89**
(iii) C Ltd					
	2019–20	**2020–21**	**2021–22**	**2022–23**	**2023–24**
Operating cash flow	2914.44	3816.83	3631.39	5118.1	6254.2
Net income	1746.22	3474.16	3506.38	4222.15	4687.03
Quality of earnings (%)	**166.90**	**109.86**	**103.57**	**121.22**	**133.40**
(iv) D Ltd					
	2019–20	**2020–21**	**2021–22**	**2022–23**	**2023–24**
Operating cash flow	1633.97	1359.7	2237	3256	3816
Net income	1243.47	1904.38	2421	3783	4470
Quality of earnings (%)	**131.40**	**71.40**	**92.40**	**86.07**	**85.37**

(v) E Ltd

	2019–20	**2020–21**	**2021–22**	**2022–23**	**2023–24**
Operating cash flow	913.91	1666.42	1912.25	2674.6	715.9
Net income	914.88	1494.82	2020.48	2842.1	3063.3
Quality of earnings (%)	**99.89**	**111.48**	**94.64**	**94.11**	**23.37**

(vi) F Ltd

	2019–20	**2020–21**	**2021–22**	**2022–23**	**2023–24**
Operating cash flow	1893.27	1851.2	1929.68	2141.19	2722.96
Net income	1592.85	2191.4	2235.35	2699.97	3120.1
Quality of earnings (%)	**118.86**	**84.48**	**86.33**	**79.30**	**87.27**

(vii) G Ltd

	2019–20	**2020–21**	**2021–22**	**2022–23**	**2023–24**
Operating cash flow	1113.33	1760.93	710.08	3336.56	2139.84
Net income	838.93	1329.36	1655.55	2564.33	2860.94
Quality of earnings (%)	**132.71**	**132.46**	**42.89**	**130.11**	**74.79**

(viii) H Ltd

	2019–20	**2020–21**	**2021–22**	**2022–23**	**2023–24**
Operating cash flow	330.41	111.6	1369.25	2130.45	1945.24
Net income	532.75	983.85	1012.14	1403.02	2173.42
Quality of earnings (%)	**62.02**	**11.34**	**135.28**	**151.85**	**89.50**

(ix) I Ltd

	2019–20	2020–21	2021–22	2022–23	2023–24
Operating cash flow	2717.53	1249.82	-221.03	2210.13	6174.5
Net income	810.34	1236.95	1528.88	1913.46	2028.92
Quality of earnings (%)	**335.36**	**101.04**	**-14.46**	**115.50**	**304.30**

(x) J Ltd

	2019–20	2020–21	2021–22	2022–23	2023–24
Operating cash flow	1169.23	1050.46	1282.26	1732.67	2091.03
Net income	779.26	885.71	863.21	1535.81	2232.6
Quality of earnings (%)	**150.04**	**118.60**	**148.55**	**112.82**	**93.66**

Appendix II

Quality of revenue for the sample companies, 2019–20 to 2023–24 *(Amount in INR crore, 1 crore = 100 million)*

(i) A Ltd.

	2019–20	**2020–21**	**2021–22**	**2022–23**	**2023–24**
Cash collected	–48.27	–737.88	–235.81	431.2	–2495.16
Sales	56247	73164.1	89124.5	118353.7	139270
Quality of revenue (%)	**–0.09**	**–1.01**	**–0.26**	**0.36**	**–1.79**

(ii) B Ltd.

	2019–20	**2020–21**	**2021–22**	**2022–23**	**2023–24**
Cash collected	–132.05	–104.86	–166.33	–338.27	82.19
Sales	3291.67	4279.05	7923.1	12457.57	13451.6
Quality of revenue (%)	**–4.01**	**–2.45**	**–2.10**	**–2.72**	**0.61**

(iii) C Ltd.

	2019–20	**2020–21**	**2021–22**	**2022–23**	**2023–24**
Cash collected	307.17	69.48	42.42	–92.23	88.15
Sales	11921	15876.9	17144.2	19762.57	22191.8
Quality of revenue (%)	**2.58**	**0.44**	**0.25**	**–0.47**	**0.40**

(iv) D Ltd.

	2019–20	**2020–21**	**2021–22**	**2022–23**	**2023–24**
Cash collected	–120.37	–620.31	–265	–774	–801
Sales	4760.89	6859.66	9028	13149	15648
Quality of revenue (%)	**–2.53**	**–9.04**	**–2.94**	**–5.89**	**–5.12**

(v) E Ltd.

	2019–20	**2020–21**	**2021–22**	**2022–23**	**2023–24**
Cash collected	–269.75	–347.25	–581.43	–614.2	–1102.7
Sales	5188.19	7276.18	10264.1	13683.9	17658.1
Quality of revenue (%)	**–5.20**	**–4.77**	**–5.66**	**–4.49**	**–6.24**

(vi) F Ltd.

	2019–20	**2020–21**	**2021–22**	**2022–23**	**2023–24**
Cash collected	–23.41	–297.61	–20.2	–88.73	–100.24
Sales	11815	13349.6	16224.4	19505.05	21355.9
Quality of revenue (%)	**–0.20**	**–2.23**	**–0.12**	**–0.45**	**–0.47**

(vii) G Ltd.

	2019–20	**2020–21**	**2021–22**	**2022–23**	**2023–24**
Cash collected	–0.37	–226.26	–461.03	–256.1	–60.52
Sales	6802.4	10480.4	12476.4	19920.09	21021.9
Quality of revenue (%)	**–0.01**	**–2.16**	**–3.70**	**–1.29**	**–0.29**

(viii) H Ltd.

	2019–20	**2020–21**	**2021–22**	**2022–23**	**2023–24**
Cash collected	–271.93	–649.02	–786.59	–690.48	–1860.37
Sales	9895.44	13362	14993.8	17935.91	25210.6
Quality of revenue (%)	**–2.75**	**–4.86**	**–5.25**	**–3.85**	**–7.38**

(ix) I Ltd.

	2019–20	**2020–21**	**2021–22**	**2022–23**	**2023–24**
Cash collected	331.11	−196.33	82.8	−65.58	−348.55
Sales	15165.9	20152	23673.4	31611.21	32885
Quality of revenue (%)	**2.18**	**−0.97**	**0.35**	**−0.21**	**−1.06**

(x) J Ltd.

	2019–20	**2020–21**	**2021–22**	**2022–23**	**2023–24**
Cash collected	−54.98	−37.38	108.56	−163.03	135.5
Sales	6129.95	7201.06	7607.2	9607.97	11551.6
Quality of revenue (%)	**−0.90**	**−0.52**	**1.43**	**−1.70**	**−1.17**

Appendix III

Beneish profit model for the sample companies 2019–20 to 2023–24

(i) A Ltd.

	2019–20	**2020–21**	**2021–22**	**2022–23**	**2023–24**
Weighted DSRI	0.75	0.81	0.71	0.55	1.16
Weighted GMI	0.67	0.79	0.97	0.86	0.82
Weighted AQI	1.05	0.66	0.3	0.87	0.88
Weighted SGI	0.81	0.93	0.87	0.95	0.84
Weighted TATA	−0.01	0	−0.01	−0.01	0
P (manipulation)	**–2.8**	**–2.88**	**–3.22**	**–2.84**	**–2.37**

(ii) B Ltd.

	2019–20	**2020–21**	**2021–22**	**2022–23**	**2023–24**
Weighted DSRI	1.05	0.85	0.62	0.83	0.69
Weighted GMI	1.27	1.73	0.35	0.95	1.48
Weighted AQI	0.73	0.7	0.43	0.57	1.22
Weighted SGI	0.99	0.93	1.33	1.13	0.77
Weighted TATA	0	−0.01	−0.02	0	0
P (manipulation)	**–2.04**	**–1.87**	**–3.36**	**–2.59**	**–1.91**

(iii) C Ltd.

	2019–20	**2020–21**	**2021–22**	**2022–23**	**2023–24**
Weighted DSRI	0.46	0.55	0.7	0.83	0.63
Weighted GMI	0.59	0.62	1	0.9	0.92

Weighted AQI	1.01	0.6	0.83	0.51	0.23
Weighted SGI	0.87	0.95	0.77	0.83	0.81
Weighted TATA	−0.01	−0.01	−0.01	−0.03	−0.04
P (manipulation)	**–3.16**	**–3.35**	**–2.77**	**–3.03**	**–3.44**

(iv) D Ltd.

	2019–20	**2020–21**	**2021–22**	**2022–23**	**2023–24**
Weighted DSRI	0.77	1.13	0.75	0.85	0.93
Weighted GMI	0.95	0.86	0.95	0.91	0.92
Weighted AQI	0.98	0.42	0.38	0.52	0.55
Weighted SGI	0.94	1.03	0.94	1.04	0.85
Weighted TATA	−0.09	−0.03	−0.06	−0.07	−0.07
P (manipulation)	**–2.51**	**–2.66**	**–3.1**	**–2.82**	**–2.89**

(v) E Ltd.

	2019–20	**2020–21**	**2021–22**	**2022–23**	**2023–24**
Weighted DSRI	0.86	0.77	0.81	0.81	0.9
Weighted GMI	1.03	0.73	0.97	0.91	1.08
Weighted AQI	0.77	0.56	0.63	0.48	0.43
Weighted SGI	0.92	1.01	1.01	0.96	0.93
Weighted TATA	−0.03	−0.01	−0.02	−0.02	−0.02
P (manipulation)	**–2.54**	**–3.01**	**–2.66**	**–2.94**	**–2.76**

(vi) F Ltd.

	2019–20	**2020–21**	**2021–22**	**2022–23**	**2023–24**
Weighted DSRI	0.85	1.66	0.7	0.79	0.87
Weighted GMI	0.87	0.88	0.9	0.91	0.9
Weighted AQI	0.92	0.63	0.48	0.54	0.53
Weighted SGI	0.77	0.81	0.87	0.86	0.79
Weighted TATA	−0.01	0	−0.01	−0.01	0.05
P (manipulation)	**−2.67**	**−2.09**	**−3.12**	**−2.98**	**−2.93**

(vii) G Ltd.

	2019–20	**2020–21**	**2021–22**	**2022–23**	**2023–24**
Weighted DSRI	0.66	0.75	1.09	0.62	0.81
Weighted GMI	0.93	0.85	0.95	0.86	1.18
Weighted AQI	0.59	0.59	0.45	0.95	0.72
Weighted SGI	0.89	1.1	0.85	1.14	0.76
Weighted TATA	−0.01	−0.01	0	−0.01	0
P (manipulation)	**−3.01**	**−2.79**	**−2.72**	**−2.51**	**−2.61**

(viii) H Ltd.

	2019–20	**2020–21**	**2021–22**	**2022–23**	**2023–24**
Weighted DSRI	0.9	0.73	0.89	0.78	0.78
Weighted GMI	0.65	0.77	0.77	0.6	0.8
Weighted AQI	0.65	0.49	0.98	0.72	0.8
Weighted SGI	0.71	0.97	0.8	0.86	1.01
Weighted TATA	−0.01	−0.01	−0.02	−0.02	−0.01
P (manipulation)	**−3.17**	**−3.12**	**−2.64**	**−3.12**	**−2.69**

(ix) I Ltd.

	2019–20	**2020–21**	**2021–22**	**2022–23**	**2023–24**
Weighted DSRI	0.37	0.81	0.62	0.67	1.14
Weighted GMI	0.32	0.98	0.88	0.85	1.04
Weighted AQI	1.05	0.44	0.43	0.85	0.87
Weighted SGI	1.03	0.95	0.84	0.96	0.75
Weighted TATA	−0.03	−0.02	−0.01	−0.01	−0.04
P (manipulation)	**−3.33**	**−2.9**	**−3.31**	**−2.76**	**−2.31**

(x) J Ltd.

	2019–20	**2020–21**	**2021–22**	**2022–23**	**2023–24**
Weighted DSRI	0.82	0.75	0.61	0.91	0.84
Weighted GMI	0.7	0.77	1.13	0.6	0.83
Weighted AQI	0.74	0.64	0.65	0.67	0.61
Weighted SGI	0.81	0.84	0.76	0.91	0.86
Weighted TATA	−0.01	0	−0.01	0	−0.01
P (manipulation)	**−3.01**	**−3.07**	**−2.93**	**−2.99**	**−2.93**

Notes: 1. Weighted ratios imply ratios with assigned weights.
2. *P* denotes the manipulation score.

GLOSSARY

Accruals: These are adjustment items and are subject to greater discretion than cash flows and show a company's accounting decision.

Altman z-score model: It is a measure of a company's financial strength that uses a weighted sum of several factors.

Asset quality index: It assesses shifts in the risk of asset realization, where an increase is seen as a sign of a greater inclination to capitalize and defer costs.

Beneish profit model: It applies a linear combination of financial variables to be converted to a "profitability manipulation."

Benford's law: It describes the relative frequency distribution of a dataset's leading digits.

Bill and hold: When products are booked as sales but delivery and ownership transfer do not take place on the day the organization records the sale, this is known as a bill and hold transaction.

Channel stuffing: It implies a business purposefully manipulating its accounting to give the impression of controlled or disciplined growth.

Costly-contracting approach: Earnings management is used to influence contractual outcomes.

Current liabilities: They are obligations whose liquidation is expected to have a maturity within one year of the operating cycle.

Day's sales in receivables index: It measures whether changes in receivables are in line with changes in sales.

Depreciation: It is a way of allocating the cost of a tangible asset over an estimated life of the asset.

Discretionary accruals: They are the accruals that are not required by business activities.

Earnings management: It is a strategy used by the management of a company to deliberately manipulate the company's earnings so the figures match a pre-determined target.

Financial shenanigans: They are actions that are taken to intentionally distort a company's reported financial performance.

Forensic accounting: It is the process of understanding, identifying, detecting, and communicating fraud patterns and schemes to stakeholders as a part of the investigation process.

Gross margin index: It analyzes whether gross margins have deteriorated, a negative signal about a firm's prospects.

Informational approach: Earnings management is used to mislead stakeholders.

Non-discretionary accruals: They are the accruals that are required by business activities.

Revenue recognition: It means that the revenues have been both realized and earned.

Roundtrip transactions: Recording business transactions between two or more companies that don't seem to have any clear business sense, goal, or financial gain.

Sales growth index: It examines growth in sales with respect to the previous year to find out whether the company is adding fake sales.

Side agreements: Sales terms and conditions modified or otherwise amended, which may impact revenue recognition.

Total accruals to total assets: It determines the extent to which earnings are cash-based, with high increases in non-cash working capital to reflect possible manipulation.

INDEX

Page numbers in *italics* indicate figures and **Bold** page numbers indicate tables in the text.

www.ingramcontent.com/pod-product-compliance
Lightning Source LLC
LaVergne TN
LVHW021131300926
849160LV00010B/971
9781041220121